THE LAW OF EQUITY COMPENSATION

A Guide to Recent Litigation and Administrative Rulings 2001–2005

ALISA J. BAKER AND COREY ROSEN

THE LAW OF EQUITY COMPENSATION

A Guide to Recent Litigation and Administrative Rulings 2001–2005

ALISA J. BAKER AND COREY ROSEN

The National Center for Employee Ownership (NCEO)
Oakland, California

This publication is designed to provide accurate and authoritative information in regard to the subject matter covered. It is sold with the understanding that the publisher is not engaged in rendering legal, accounting, or other professional service. If legal advice or other expert assistance is required, the services of a competent professional person should be sought.

Legal, accounting, and other rules affecting business often change. Before making decisions based on the information you find here or in any publication from any publisher, you should ascertain what changes might have occurred and what changes might be forthcoming. The NCEO's Web site (including the members-only area) and newsletter for members provide regular updates on these changes. If you have any questions or concerns about a particular issue, check with your professional advisor or, if you are an NCEO member, call or email us.

The Law of Equity Compensation
Alisa J. Baker and Corey Rosen
Editing and book design by Scott S. Rodrick

Copyright © 2006 by The National Center for Employee Ownership. All rights reserved. Printed in the United States of America. No part of this book may be reproduced or transmitted in any form or by any means, electronic or mechanical, including photocopying, recording, or by any information storage and retrieval system, without prior written permission from the publisher.

The National Center for Employee Ownership
1736 Franklin Street, 8th Floor
Oakland, CA 94612
(510) 208-1300
(510) 272-9510 (fax)
Web site: http://www.nceo.org/

ISBN: 1-932924-24-8

Summary Table of Contents

Preface xv

Introduction xvii

Part I: Litigation Review

1. **General Contract Interpretation and Implementation Issues** 3
   1. Waiver, Oral Modification, and Related Claims 5
   2. Inconsistent Documents and Ambiguous Language 9
   3. Ignorance Is Not Bliss 13
   4. Miscellaneous Contract Issues 15

2. **Equity Issues Related to Employment Disputes** 19
   1. Recent Cases on the Effects of Termination 20
   2. Options as Wages 22
   3. Noncompete Agreements and Stock Option Forfeitures 25
   4. Calculating Damages When the Breach of an Equity Agreement Is Related to Termination 29

3. **Treatment of Equity in Corporate Transactions** 33
   1. Change-in-Control Date Issues 34
   2. Exercise After Spin-Off or Divestiture 36

4. **Choice of Law Issues** 39
   1. Disputes Implicating International Issues 40
   2. Federal/State Preemption Issues 41
   3. Stock Options in Bankruptcy Claims 44
   4. Miscellaneous 46

5. **Allocation of Equity Rights Under Family Law** 47
   Arizona 49
   Arkansas 50

vi | The Law of Equity Compensation

    California 50

    Connecticut 51

    Florida 52

    Maryland 53

    Massachusetts 53

    Minnesota 53

    Missouri 54

    New Hampshire 55

    New Jersey 55

    North Carolina 56

    Ohio 57

    Pennsylvania 57

    Washington 58

6. **Tax Litigation Arising from Equity Compensation Issues** 61
    1. U.S. Tax Court Rulings 62
    2. State Tax Law Issues 65

Part II: Recent Administrative Rulings and Regulations

7. **IRS Rulings on Equity Compensation** 71
    1. Corporate Matters 72
    2. Individual Matters 75
    3. Stock Plan Administration 79
    4. Section 423 ESPPs 81
    5. Tax Shelters 84

8. **Final and Proposed Tax Regulations** 87
    1. Section 409A Deferred Compensation Rules 88
    2. Final Regulations for Statutory Stock Options 97

9. **Securities Law Legislation and Rulings** 105
    1. The Sarbanes-Oxley Act of 2002 106
    2. SEC Rulings and No-Action Letters 114

Part III: Table of Cases

Table of Cases 135

About the Authors 141

About Levine & Baker LLP 143

About the NCEO 145

(Full table of contents follows on next page)

Contents

Preface xv

Introduction xvii

Part I: Litigation Review

1. **General Contract Interpretation and Implementation Issues** 3
    1. Waiver, Oral Modification, and Related Claims 5

        Failure to follow plan procedure by exercising in writing is fatal to claim, even if documents were ambiguous as to post-termination exercise period 5

        Even when agreements are clear, oral representations may result in extended post-termination exercise period 6

        Employee's continuing employment indicated agreement to modification of option grant 7

        Employer waived buyback rights by failure to timely respond to information requests 7

        Employer's failure to observe post-termination exercise periods may result in a waiver of the terms of the plan 8

    2. Inconsistent Documents and Ambiguous Language 9

        Ambiguity of provisions regarding post-termination exercise period do not overcome failure to follow plan procedure by exercising in writing 10

        Inconsistencies between general memorandum and specific option agreements are resolved in favor of option agreement 10

        Option acceleration language resolved with reference to whole agreement 11

        Insufficient definition of "cause" results in common meaning 11

        Ambiguous use of term "participation" in employment agreement interpreted in accordance with terms of stock incentive plan under Delaware law 12

    3. Ignorance Is Not Bliss 13

        No right to exercise options when reasonable reliance on company misrepresentations could have been cured by reading accurate statements 13

        No right to additional vesting when misunderstanding could have been corrected by reading plan document 14

    4. Miscellaneous Contract Issues 15

        Generally, oral promises to grant options are unenforceable 15

        But a written promise to grant equity rights (particularly phantom stock) may be enforceable even if specific grants were never made............16

        You take your risks with equity compensation 16

2. **Equity Issues Related to Employment Disputes** **19**

    1. Recent Cases on the Effects of Termination 20

        Right of repurchase for unvested shares on termination valid 20

        Post-termination exercise period cannot begin until employee knows he is terminated 21

    2. Options as Wages...22

        Stock options not wages under Maryland law..22

        Idaho court must rule on whether options are wages..............................23

        Inclusion of stock option gains for purposes of calculating retirement plan benefits is based on past practice..24

    3. Noncompete Agreements and Stock Option Forfeitures 25

        Choice of law on noncompetes governs enforceability of stock option forfeiture clause..25

        Strange goings-on in Texas: Unenforceable noncompete, enforceable forfeiture 26

        Forfeiture clauses: A note of caution to companies that do business in California 27

    4. Calculating Damages When the Breach of an Equity Agreement Is Related to Termination 29

        Value of stock option damages measured as of date option agreement breached 30

        Value of stock option damages measured as of date of wrongful termination 30

3. **Treatment of Equity in Corporate Transactions** **33**

    1. Change-in-Control Date Issues 34

        Acceleration of vesting triggered only if merger is actually completed........34

        Employees who terminate after merger agreement signed but before stockholder approval obtained are not entitled to acceleration................34

        Sale of bankrupt company's assets triggers change in control......................35

x | The Law of Equity Compensation

    2. Exercise After Spin-Off or Divestiture 36
        Sale of subsidiary constitutes a termination of employment for purposes of stock option plan 36

4. **Choice of Law Issues** 39
   1. Disputes Implicating International Issues 40
      - Choice of California law in stock option agreement governs notwithstanding employment agreement 40
      - U.S. seizure of options not unlawful..41
   2. Federal/State Preemption Issues..41
      - Federal securities law preempts state fraud claims concerning option value 42
      - Stock plan incentives may give rise to securities fraud..42
      - Original filing under ERISA not fatal to phantom stock contract claims.......43
   3. Stock Options in Bankruptcy Claims..44
      - Employee claim to payment under option agreement partially allowed as post-petition administrative priority of Chapter 11 bankruptcy estate..44
      - Stock options partially exempt from Chapter 7 bankruptcy claims...............45
      - Unvested options subject to bankruptcy claims..45
   4. Miscellaneous..46
      - Insurance coverage 46
      - Arbitration 46

5. **Allocation of Equity Rights Under Family Law** 47
   - Arizona 49
     - Employer's intent a critical issue in dividing options..49
     - Vested options count for child support..49
   - Arkansas 50
     - Income from future stock options includable in alimony settlement 50
   - California..50
     - Exercised stock options are includible in child support calculations 50
     - Extra year added to time rule to account for vesting 51
   - Connecticut 51
     - Post-separation, pre-dissolution options are marital property..51
     - Unvested options not marital assets..52

Contents | xi

Florida 52
Stock options for future performance are not spouse's separate property 52

Maryland 53
Both vested and unvested options may be subject to division 53

Massachusetts 53
Unvested options are assets includible in marital estate 53

Minnesota 53
Trial court has broad discretion to value options 53

Missouri 54
Stock options granted the day after divorce becomes final are not subject to division in divorce settlement 54
Options awarded before dissolution are marital property, even if unvested 54

New Hampshire 55
Unvested options divided according to when they were earned 55

New Jersey 55
Wife not entitled to half of options granted just before divorce 55
Stock options granted after divorce excludable from child support calculation 56

North Carolina 56
Court allows intrinsic value method for options in divorce case 56

Ohio 57
Stock options granted during marriage are subject to division 57

Pennsylvania 57
Parent's income includes unexercised vested options 57
Unvested options are marital assets 57

Washington 58
Stock option proceeds deposited in various investment accounts marital property 58
Options are community property, including increase in share value post-exercise 59
Options valued as of date of vesting 60

xii | The Law of Equity Compensation

6. Tax Litigation Arising from Equity Compensation Issues 61

    1. U.S. Tax Court Rulings 62

        IRS need not compromise on AMT liability 62

        Exercise of option with third-party loan does not eliminate tax consequences under Section 83 63

        Blackout trading period not a substantial risk of forfeiture 64

        Tax on option exercise unaffected by Section 16 64

    2. State Tax Law Issues 65

        California: Disposition of options by nonresident subject to California tax.....65

        California: Taxes must be paid by nonresident on exercised options 66

        California: Stock transfer occurs notwithstanding margin loan 66

        New York: Gain on stock options must be allocated between New York and Washington...67

        New York: Nonresident's stock payments ruled to be New York source income 68

Part II: Recent Administrative Rulings and Regulations

7. IRS Rulings on Equity Compensation 71

    1. Corporate Matters...72

        Rev. Rul. 2003-98: Deductibility of options after grantor company is acquired 73

        Notice 2005-99: Restricted stock and restricted stock units can be accounted for under cost-sharing arrangements 73

        Rec. Rul. 2001-1: Corporate deductions for exercise of nonqualified options not subject to AMT...74

        PLR 200550007: Cashless exercise program does not affect Section 162(m) calculation...74

    2. Individual Matters...75

        Rev. Rul. 2005-48: Income from options must be recognized despite stock sale restrictions 75

        Rev. Rul. 2004-60, Rev. Rul. 2002-22, and Notice 2002-31: Transfers of nonstatutory stock options and nonqualified deferred compensation pursuant to divorce...76

        Rev. Rul. 2004-37: IRS issues ruling on reducing debt under promissory notes used for option exercise 78

Contents | xiii

      PLR 200032017: Vested nonqualified stock options are not parachute payments 79

   3. Stock Plan Administration 79

      Rev. Rul. 2004-60: Transfer of options in divorce 79

      PLR 200551015: Amendment to ISO plan does not require shareholder approval 79

      PLR 200513012: Incentive stock option plan with ESPP-like features qualifies 80

      Rev. Proc. 2002-50: IRS exempts brokers from certain stock option reporting requirements 80

      PLR 200207005: IRS allows paperless exercise of options 81

   4. Section 423 ESPPs 81

      PLR 200547007: Amendment to ESPP excluding non–W-2 employees does not affect plan qualification 81

      PLR 200418020: Reduction in offering period not a "modification" 82

      PLR 200241001: Date of grant in an ESPP is start of offering period even if employee buys shares with a lump-sum payment 82

      PLR 200244006: ESPP can offer special purchase and entry dates to accommodate merger without shareholder approval 83

      PLR 200102042: Plan that has a first refusal right qualifies under Section 423 83

   5. Tax Shelters 84

      Announcement 2005-19: Settlement initiative for stock option tax shelter scheme 84

      Rev. Rul. 2004-37: IRS shuts down purchase price adjustment scheme 85

8. **Final and Proposed Tax Regulations** **87**

   1. Section 409A Deferred Compensation Rules...88

      Notice 2005-1 and proposed regulations under 409A: Specific application of the new rules to equity awards 88

      Overview of coverage 89

      General application of the new rules..89

      Specific application of the new rules to equity awards 90

      Valuation requirements for options and SARs 93

      Timeline for compliance 96

      2005 transition rules 96

xiv | The Law of Equity Compensation

    2. Final Regulations for Statutory Stock Options 97
       Final statutory stock option regulations: Treasury Regulations
       Sections 1.421-424 97
       Final regulations for option transfers to related parties under
       Section 83 103

9. Securities Law Legislation and Rulings 105
    1. The Sarbanes-Oxley Act of 2002 106
       Prohibition on personal loans to directors and executive officers 106
       Accelerated Section 16 filing deadlines 109
       Foreign private issuers 110
       SEC rulemaking 110
       Recommendations 112
       Forfeiture of compensation and stock sale profits by CEOs and CFOs
       upon restatements due to misconduct 113
       Freeze on extraordinary payments to directors and officers 114
    2. SEC Rulings and No-Action Letters 114
       Accounting issues 115
       Plan operations 117
       Registration exemptions 120
       Reporting and disclosure issues 121
       Shareholder rights 122
       Stock exchange rulings 130

Part III: Table of Cases

Table of Cases 135

About the Authors 141

About Levine & Baker LLP 143

About the NCEO 145

Preface

In recent years, the NCEO's *Journal of Employee Ownership Law and Finance* has published an annual update on equity compensation-related litigation. The annual update has provided a useful snapshot of the issues that arise in this complex area of the law. However, given the sheer volume of case law devoted to equity compensation since the turn of the century, it seemed the time had come to take a more comprehensive view of litigation trends. This volume represents our attempt to review and organize significant case law and regulatory developments in equity compensation during the years 2001 to 2005. We plan to issue a new edition each year, updated to incorporate developments since the last edition.

The book focuses on cases and rulings that affect two key areas: broad-based equity plans and executive equity agreements. Part I, "Litigation Review," is organized in standard legal format with the aim of providing research assistance to the practitioner. Key court cases are summarized, with supporting (or opposing) authorities noted as appropriate. Part II, "Recent Administrative Rulings and Regulations," is more narrative and covers agency rulings in a less formal way. All chapters are organized by subject matter, with most chapters providing a brief introduction and issue overview for your convenience.

We hope this volume will give users an indication of the direction of the law and the various approaches being taken by the courts (and litigants) to resolving disputes involving equity compensation. Please note that our intention is to concentrate on the aspects of these decisions that we believe to be most relevant to the concerns of our audience, and thus our editorial judgment on this is highly subjective. Our case summaries and analyses are intended as tools only; always read (and update) the primary sources before relying on anything in the text.

A Note on Sources and Citation

The decisions reviewed in the text come from federal, state, and local courts, as well as from regulatory agencies (particularly the Internal

Revenue Service [IRS] and the Securities and Exchange Commission). Whenever practical, we use the official citation for cases. In some cases, the official citation is unavailable, and we refer to unofficial sources (including LEXIS). In some cases we cite to unpublished (but available) cases. Please note that unpublished cases are not citable as precedent in all jurisdictions, and their value is primarily as an indication of trends in the law. Also note that many of the decisions reviewed below are judicial orders on a motion for summary judgment by one (or both) of the parties. That is, they are rulings on whether the facts raise sufficient issues of law to merit further consideration by a judge or jury. It is important not to confuse such rulings with substantive opinions on the law (e.g., that an issue must be resolved in a certain way).

Federal tax decisions and rulings have their own specific form of citation and precedental value. Published IRS revenue rulings, regulations, and procedures represent the IRS position on tax issues. Unpublished rulings (such as private letter rulings, technical advice memoranda, and field service memoranda) are binding only as issued to a specific taxpayer and are not cited as law. However, as with unpublished legal opinions, such rulings are helpful for providing taxpayers with an indication of the IRS views on current issues.

Please let us know if you have questions or comments for the next edition.

Alisa J. Baker
Corey Rosen

Summer 2006

Our gratitude, as always, to Scott Rodrick at NCEO for his expert editorial guidance. And special thanks to Rick Levine and Kurt Bodden at Levine & Baker LLP for their generous input, patience, and support during this project.

INTRODUCTION

The years between 2001 and 2005 were very busy ones for lawyers and consultants who work with equity compensation. Growing unease about the way stock options and other equity compensation plans had been used during the late 1990s and the first several years of the twenty-first century were reflected in major changes to accounting rules, equity plan disclosure requirements, and stock exchange rules. These concerns continue to this day. On the accounting front, U.S. and international accounting bodies now require that companies record the present value of equity awards on their income statements. The Securities and Exchange Commission (SEC) instituted new rules to let users of financial statements see how much equity, and in what form, is being provided to employees each year. At the end of 2005, the SEC signaled its intentions to make these rules even more detailed for executive equity compensation. Major stock exchanges created new and stricter rules for shareholder approval of equity plans, requiring, among other things, approvals of plan modifications and requiring that shares held in street name by brokers only be voted with specific instructions from shareholders.

In 2004 and 2005, important changes were made to the tax treatment of deferred compensation plans. As a rule, employees now must specify well in advance a date to which deferral of an award will be made, unless the award is granted in the event of death, disability, termination, or retirement. Serious tax consequences follow a failure to comply with the rules. While most kinds of equity compensation (stock options and stock appreciation rights issued at fair market value, and restricted stock awards) are generally exempt from the new rules, phantom stock and restricted stock units are covered. Rules detailing how to determine fair market value were issued in 2005, but they await further clarification.

As always, there were many claims for employee equity award benefits litigated in the courts. Several major themes emerged. Claims that equity awards were subject to the Employee Retirement Income Security Act (ERISA) were uniformly denied. Disputes over conflicts between oral representations and written documents generally favored the documents, although some company behavior patterns could overrule this. Change-in-control transactions raised issues with regard to vesting and acceleration. Non-compete agreements continued to be controversial, and courts have been divided on just how aggressively they can be enforced with equity awards.

Divorce cases showed an inconsistent pattern of rulings. Because the issues are subject to state law, there have been varying decisions about how to divide unvested options. The "time rule" that looks to when the employee was actually working for the company and covered by the awards during the marriage is the most frequently used allocation method.

On tax issues, legislation was passed in 2004 to permanently exclude withholding on disqualifying dispositions of incentive stock options and Section 423 employee stock purchase plan (ESPP) options. Comprehensive regulations for incentive stock options were issued, dealing with such issues as how to determine fair market value, plan modifications, and change-in-control transactions. The IRS also issued final rules on qualified cost-sharing arrangements and equity compensation, as well as final transfer regulations for nonstatutory options.

The SEC tightened restrictions as to when companies may disallow shareholder votes on options, reversing prior rulings allowing most of these proposals to be excluded under the "ordinary business" exception. The Sarbanes-Oxley Act introduced a major overhaul of corporate governance and reporting rules, some of which affects how equity compensation is awarded.

As we go to press, the national media is focused on apparent abuses involving alleged illegal stock option backdating practices by many public companies. The drumbeat goes on, and the result will be reviewed in the next update to this volume.

A note on what we have not included in this volume: Changes in accounting rules generated the most controversy, but we have chosen not to provide substantial detail on this issue here. The NCEO publishes a comprehensive book on the subject titled *Accounting for Equity Compensation Plans*. Further, because of the many statutory and regulatory changes that are now in process with respect to federal securities laws, we have largely excluded securities law litigation from Part I. The landscape has changed drastically for such lawsuits, and we believe it makes the most sense to take a "wait and see" approach for the time being.

Part I:
Litigation Review

CHAPTER 1

General Contract Interpretation and Implementation Issues

Contents

1. **Waiver, Oral Modification, and Related Claims** 5

    Failure to follow plan procedure by exercising in writing is fatal to claim, even if documents were ambiguous as to post-termination exercise period 5

    Even when agreements are clear, oral representations may result in extended post-termination exercise period 6

    Employee's continuing employment indicated agreement to modification of option grant 7

    Employer waived buyback rights by failure to timely respond to information requests 7

    Employer's failure to observe post-termination exercise periods may result in a waiver of the terms of the plan 8

2. **Inconsistent Documents and Ambiguous Language** 9

    Ambiguity of provisions regarding post-termination exercise period do not overcome failure to follow plan procedure by exercising in writing 10

    Inconsistencies between general memorandum and specific option agreements are resolved in favor of option agreement 10

    Option acceleration language resolved with reference to whole agreement 11

    Insufficient definition of "cause" results in common meaning 11

    Ambiguous use of term "participation" in employment agreement interpreted in accordance with terms of stock incentive plan under Delaware law 12

3. Ignorance Is Not Bliss 13
No right to exercise options when reasonable reliance on company misrepresentations could have been cured by reading accurate statements 13
No right to additional vesting when misunderstanding could have been corrected by reading plan document 14

4. Miscellaneous Contract Issues 15
Generally, oral promises to grant options are unenforceable 15
But a written promise to grant equity rights (particularly phantom stock) may be enforceable even if specific grants were never made 16
You take your risks with equity compensation 16

For all its technical specificity, the law applicable to employee stock rights is essentially contract law. So it is not surprising that the bulk of equity compensation litigation arises from disagreement over the meaning of the plan, grant, or other controlling document: i.e., a contract dispute. For example, an inartfully drafted or ambiguous document may give confusing guidance—or no guidance at all—as to the treatment of equity rights in a change of control situation. Key terms may be undefined or inadequately defined. Oral representations may conflict with written documentation. As with any contract, the potential issues are limitless, and judicial decisions will be based on the specific facts of each situation. Further, in most contract cases, state law—rather than federal law—will control, and so the results may differ on the same facts from jurisdiction to jurisdiction.

As will be seen from the cases below, whenever possible, courts will do their best to defer to a written document. However, the issuer (which is generally the drafter) cannot expect to rely on its own discretion in interpreting ambiguous language: the employee's understanding of his or her rights will also be considered by the courts. If a company's actions are inconsistent with its documents, those actions may well support a reading of the document that supports the actions, rather than vice versa. Ignorance of plan documents—by either party—is not an excuse.

Employers that enter into equity arrangements cannot be too careful when drafting documents that relate or make reference to equity grants. Inconsistencies, ambiguities, or oral representations that vary from the writings are invitations to litigation. On the employee side, reading and understanding all equity documents is a must. The documents to be reviewed include the plan as well as any individual executive agreements that could have a bearing on employee rights. There is no benefit to hoping for the best and then waiting to see what happens at the time of exercise.

1. Waiver, Oral Modification, and Related Claims

When do words or actions modify a written option agreement? This is a highly fact-specific inquiry. Although a plain reading of the documents usually prevails, whenever there is ambiguity, either party can sabotage a document by its behavior, including its oral communications.

Failure to follow plan procedure by exercising in writing is fatal to claim, even if documents were ambiguous as to post-termination exercise period

In *Donaldson v. Digital General Systems*, 168 S.W.3d 909 (Tex. App.-5th July 22, 2005), before plaintiff Donaldson's termination of employment, he negotiated a transition agreement with employer Digital General Systems (DGS) that purported to extend his post-termination exercise period from 30 days to one year. The agreement cross-referenced the DGS option plan as the governing document with respect to option terms. The plan document provided a default post-term exercise period of 30 days and a maximum of six months. Six months after his termination, Donaldson called the DGS option administrator to explore exercising and was advised that his options had expired one month after his termination. Donaldson argued in state court that DGS had breached its contract with him by refusing to let him exercise within the one-year period. The trial court held that while the language of the documents was ambiguous, Donaldson's failure to submit a written exercise notice in and of itself invalidated his claim that DGS had failed to honor his exercise.

Held: On appeal to the Texas Court of Appeals, affirmed for defendant DGS. Donaldson's failure to submit a written exercise notice in accordance with the terms of the option agreement was not excused by his conversation with DGS (to the effect that his options had expired). He had previously exercised three options, each time on the same written form, and he was aware of the requirements to do so in writing.

See also Applewhite v. Computer Associates International, 3-01CV0853-R (N.D. Tex. Apr. 18, 2002) (order denying a motion for summary judgment on the issue of whether plaintiff's failure to present a written notice of exercise invalidated his breach of contract claim). *But cf. D'Oliveira v. Rare Hospitality Int'l Inc.*, 2003 R.I. Super. LEXIS 28 (Feb. 13, 2003) (under New York law, no need to attempt to exercise in writing if employer has made it clear that it will reject the attempt); *Noguchi v. Guidant Corp.*, 2002 Cal. App. Unpub. LEXIS 10210 (Nov. 5, 2002) (statements made by HR representative to terminating employee may modify contract such that failure to exercise in writing will not preclude effective exercise of option).

Even when agreements are clear, oral representations may result in extended post-termination exercise period

In *Moses v. Corning Inc.*, No. 03-3003 (3rd Cir. July 16, 2004) (unpublished), plaintiff Moses was an executive in a Corning subsidiary that was spun off as an independent company in 1996. Although his options, on their terms, would have expired at the time of the spin-off, Corning amended them in writing to extend their exercise period through his termination date at the new company. Moses subsequently attempted to exercise the options two years after his termination date, claiming that a representative of the Corning legal department had told him that he could exercise his options for an extended period after termination. Corning rejected the exercise, and Moses sued for breach of contract and promissory estoppel based on the oral modification.

Held: On appeal to the U.S. Court of Appeals for the Third Circuit, summary judgment affirmed for Corning on breach of contract; remand with respect to promissory estoppel on the oral representations. The appellate court saw no ambiguity in the writing itself, but it concluded that the in-house counsel's comments could have given rise to reasonable reliance on an extended post-termination exercise period.

See also Levy v. Lucent Techs. Inc., 2003 U.S. Dist. LEXIS 414 (S.D.N.Y. Jan. 14, 2003) (oral representations to executive by HR representative could constitute enforceable promise to accelerate vesting); *Bailey v. Grey, Siefert & Co., Inc.*, 752 N.Y.S. 2d 646 (N.Y. App. Div.-1st Dec. 31, 2002) (no oral modification when representative not authorized to modify option agreement). *Cf. Ingram v. Rencor Controls, Inc.*, No. 02-58-P-C (D. Me. Apr. 11, 2003) (plaintiff's claim that there was an oral agreement for him to receive 10% of the stock of his employer barred by Maine statute of limitations, which requires agreements that cannot be performed in one year to be in writing).

Employee's continuing employment indicated agreement to modification of option grant

In *Cochran v. Quest Software*, 328 F.3d 1 (1st Cir. 2003), plaintiff Cochran was an at-will employee who received an option grant at hire, subject to standard vesting at the rate of 25% per year under the terms of the Quest option plan. During Cochran's first year of employment (and before any options had vested), he was advised that his grant was being reduced due to his poor job performance. Notwithstanding the reduction, Cochran continued to work at the company. At the end of his first year his employment was terminated, and when he exercised his option, it was for the reduced number of vested shares. Among other things, Cochran sued for breach of contract on a theory the option had been unilaterally rescinded by Quest. On a motion for summary judgment, the U.S. District Court for Massachusetts held in favor of defendant on all counts and dismissed the claims.

Held: On appeal to the U.S. Court of Appeals for the First Circuit, affirmed in favor of defendant. The appellate court upheld the trial court's finding that Cochran's behavior evidenced agreement to the modification of his option agreement; i.e., he voluntarily continued his at-will employment at Quest even after he knew about the reduction. Under Massachusetts law, options are not earned until vested. Thus, the reduction of the number of shares granted before the completion of the plaintiff's first year of employment was not (without more) a breach of contract.

Employer waived buyback rights by failure to timely respond to information requests

In *Medtronic Inc. v. Wohlfeld*, 2002 WL 523873 (D. Minn. Mar. 23, 2002), plaintiff Medtronic sued for equitable relief when its former employee

Wohlfeld refused to sell Medtronic shares back to the company after he went to work for a competitor.

Under Medtronic's option plan, Medtronic had a right to repurchase shares at their original exercise price from any employee who joined a competitor within six months after termination of his or her employment at Medtronic. Wohlfeld, who was a national group marketing director, exercised his options in 1997 and then joined a competing company. Two months later, Medtronic's director of shareholder services sent Wohlfeld a letter saying the company was exercising its repurchase rights. Wohlfeld's attorney sent back a request asking for more information. Fifteen months after that, Wohlfeld received a demand letter for the shares from the company. Another six months went by before the company filed a lawsuit in federal court asking for an order that Wohlfeld return the shares and pay damages equal to the highest value of the shares during the period in dispute. In response, Wohlfeld argued that the company should be equitably estopped from exercising its rights because Medtronic willfully misrepresented its rules and procedures on this issue. He claimed that he was told by a supervisor that his plan of joining a competitor would not result in adverse legal consequences. Further, the company's failure to respond to his information requests had resulted in his belief that the stock was not actually subject to repurchase.

Held: Summary judgment in favor of defendant Wohlfeld. By failing to respond to Wohlfeld's requests for information for 20 months, the company created an "unconscionable" situation and waived its (otherwise valid) rights to repurchase.

See also *Crampton v. Abbott Laboratories*, 186 F. Supp. 2d 850 (N.D. Ill. 2002) (company could not refuse to permit exercise of options based on employee's failure to sign noncompete verification form at termination when it never provided her with the form).

Employer's failure to observe post-termination exercise periods may result in a waiver of the terms of the plan

In *Snyder v. Time Warner*, 179 F. Supp. 2d 1374 (N.D. Ga. 2001), plaintiff Snyder was a former employee of TBS, which was acquired by Time Warner (TWI) in 1996. At the time of the acquisition, all of Snyder's options in TBS accelerated. Both the TBS plan and the individual option agreements provided for a 90-day post-termination exercise period.

Snyder's employment terminated on July 1, 1997. At that time, he asked TWI for clarification on his post-termination exercise period. In response to his request, he received on August 14, 1997, a written stock option status report from TWI giving specific expiration dates for the options ranging from 2003 to 2006. He also received a memo from TWI about its captive broker arrangement with PaineWebber, including exercise information. In October 1998 Snyder exercised for 500 shares and received a confirming report. In July 1999, he tried to exercise for 250 shares and was told at that time that his options had actually expired on October 1, 1997 (90 days after his termination). Snyder then filed an action for breach of contract, fraud, promissory estoppel, and negligent misrepresentation. TWI filed a motion for summary judgment on all claims.

Held: Motion for summary judgment denied. Under Georgia law, the language of a contract may be varied by mutual consent. TWI's acceptance of the payment for the first exercise—combined with furnishing the initial report, the broker information, and the confirming report—could support a jury finding on mutuality and if not on mutuality, then on waiver of the post-termination exercise period. Similarly, the jury could find for Snyder on promissory estoppel, since the reports were highly specific as to the exercise period and there could certainly have been reasonable, justifiable reliance on them by Snyder. Finally, the jury could find that TWI negligently misrepresented the period to Snyder to his detriment.

2. Inconsistent Documents and Ambiguous Language

Equity arrangements frequently involve a number of different documents, which may include a plan, individual grant agreements, and, at the executive level, employment and stock purchase agreements. If all documents are not harmonized, or if they cross-reference inconsistent provisions, the situation becomes an invitation to litigation. The problem is often exacerbated by oral representations made between the parties, evidence of which may come in at trial if the writings are unclear.

Ambiguity of provisions regarding post-termination exercise period do not overcome failure to follow plan procedure by exercising in writing

In *Donaldson v. Digital General Systems*, 168 S.W.3d 909 (Tex. App.-5th July 22, 2005), plaintiff Donaldson, as noted in the discussion of this case above, negotiated a transition agreement after a change in control to his employer, DGS. The agreement purported to grant him additional options and to provide a one-year post-termination exercise period instead of the usual 30 days. However, the same agreement cross-referenced the DGS stock plan as the governing document. The plan did not on its face authorize extended post-term exercise periods of more than six months. Extrinsic evidence on what the parties had intended at the time of negotiating the agreement was inconclusive. In this instance, the appellate court was able to finesse the issue by deciding the case on the failure to exercise in writing (see above). Given the specific language of the transition agreement and the conflicting testimony of the parties, it is not clear which way this would have gone without the procedural exercise issue.

Inconsistencies between general memorandum and specific option agreements are resolved in favor of option agreement

In *First Marblehead Corp. v. House*, 401 F. Supp. 2d 152 (D. Mass. 2005), House was an executive for First Marblehead who had experience as a trader and analyst of traded stock options before joining the firm. He assisted in setting up the company's option plan and was granted options. During his employment, House received a general memorandum from company counsel that described the terms of the plan (including a 10-year exercise period) but gave no details regarding post-termination exercise. When formal documentation was ultimately adopted, both the plan document and the grant agreements expressly stated that options must be exercised within 90 days of termination.

House terminated his employment in 1998 without exercising his options. At the time of his termination, he did not review (and claims not to have received) his option agreements. Six years later, he attempted to exercise his vested options. The company filed for declaratory relief that the exercise was invalid, and House counterclaimed for breach of contract.

Held: Summary judgment in favor of First Marblehead. The U.S. District Court rejected House's argument that the company was bound by a generic overview rather than by the specific agreement. The court also noted that House was no "babe in the woods" and should have known to inquire about when to exercise his options after termination.

Option acceleration language resolved with reference to whole agreement

In *Sanchez v. Verio, Inc.*, No. 01-11341 (5th Cir. Dec. 27, 2004) (unpublished), plaintiff Sanchez was employed by Verio from 1998 to 2000, receiving four option grants during that period, each of which vested at the rate of 25% per year during her employment. Her option agreement provided that options would fully vest if she was "terminated by the company or related entity without cause or by the optionee with good reason within 12 months of a change in control." At the time of Sanchez's termination, Verio was in M&A discussions, but the merger was not completed until 4 months after Sanchez left the company. Sanchez then attempted to exercise her unvested options based on the theory that the merger occurred "within 12 months" of her termination. The company rejected the exercise, arguing that notwithstanding the use of the word "within," acceleration could occur only while Sanchez was actually an employee of the company, which was not the case at the time of the change in control. Sanchez sued for breach of contract, and the jury found that because the language was ambiguous, the option should have vested in full as of the change in control.

Held: Reversed by U.S. Court of Appeals for the Fifth Circuit. The appellate court determined that notwithstanding the use of the word "within," the language regarding timing of acceleration was unambiguous. Under the terms of the option, vesting could occur only during the optionee's employment at Verio. Sanchez was not employed at the time of the change in control, so no acceleration was possible.

Insufficient definition of "cause" results in common meaning

In *Scribner v. WorldCom, Inc.*, 249 F.3d 902 (9th Cir. 2001), plaintiff Scribner was terminated from WorldCom as a result of the spin-off of his division. Upon termination, he attempted to exercise his options. The company refused to honor the exercise based on its ability under the stock option plan to cancel options when an employee was terminated with cause. The plan did not have a definition of "cause" but instead left its determination to the employer's discretion. WorldCom claimed that termination in connection with a divestiture was termination "with cause." The U.S. District Court for the Eastern District of Washington granted summary judgment in favor of WorldCom.

Held: On appeal to the U.S. Court of Appeals for the Fifth Circuit, reversed and remanded with instructions to enter summary judgment in favor of Scribner. The appellate court held that without a specific plan definition, "cause" must be given its common employment law meaning. Under Washington state law, this includes "some shortcoming on the part of the employee." WorldCom conceded there was no such a shortcoming in Scribner's case. The court concluded that WorldCom had a duty to interpret the terms in good faith, not to simply define the term in the way most favorable and convenient to the company.

See also *Seraphine v. Aqua Bath Co.*, 2003 Tenn. App. LEXIS (Tenn. Ct. App. 248 Mar. 28, 2003) (limit on post-termination exercise period cannot be read in by employer when not included in written option agreement); *Roller v. Chrysler Corporation*, No. 227523 (Mich. Ct. App. Jun. 7, 2002) (unpublished) (difference between "retirement" in stock option agreement and "lay-off" in separation agreement must be resolved by court to determine length of post-termination exercise period).

Ambiguous use of term "participation" in employment agreement interpreted in accordance with terms of stock incentive plan under Delaware law

In *Gelhaus v. Fingerhut Companies, Inc.* (Minn. Ct. App. May 7, 2002) (unpublished), plaintiff Gelhaus was president of a subsidiary of Fingerhut. His employment agreement with Fingerhut stated that he was entitled to "participate in" benefit plans offered to executives, including stock options, and he received Fingerhut options through 1995. During this period, he and the company disputed whether he was an employee of Fingerhut or of the subsidiary. Although Fingerhut advised him that his employer was the subsidiary rather than the parent company, Gelhaus continued to maintain—while still working for the subsidiary—that his employment agreement with Fingerhut was ongoing. In 1999, Federated Department Stores acquired Fingerhut, and Gelhaus sued for breach of contract based on (among other things) Fingerhut's failure to grant him additional stock options in the company during the prior four-year period. He argued that the language of the employment contract required that he participate in the stock plan—i.e., that he receive stock options each year. The trial court granted summary judgment to Fingerhut.

Held: Affirmed on appeal to the Minnesota Court of Appeals. The appellate court agreed with the trial court that, even if the employment agreement was in place, its language was too ambiguous to construe without reference to the stock plan documents. Those documents gave absolute discretion to the compensation committee to select which participants received options in any given year.

3. Ignorance Is Not Bliss

Disputes over equity grants often arise because—notwithstanding the documents—the parties have different understandings of their rights. This is particularly common in the context of termination after a change in control or other corporate transaction, when questions raised by an optionee may be answered off-the-cuff by company representatives. Generally, courts are not sympathetic to the argument that an optionee relied to his detriment on rights he believed he had when those rights were not set out in the documents. This conclusion is particularly likely when the optionee is an executive or other option-savvy employee.

No right to exercise options when reasonable reliance on company misrepresentations could have been cured by reading accurate statements

In *Vague v. Bank One Corporation*, C.A. No. 18741-NC (Del. Ch. Ct. 2003), *reversed and remanded* (Del. May 20, 2004), C.A. No. 18741-NC (Del. Ch. Ct. Feb 1, 2006), plaintiff Vague earned, through his employment with First USA, a predecessor of Bank One, the right to exercise two options to acquire Bank One stock. As a result of conversations that occurred in connection with his employment termination after the merger, Vague mistakenly believed he had a few extra years to exercise under the options, and so he failed to exercise until eight months after they had expired in August 2000. Bank One rejected his effort to exercise, and Vague sued in Delaware Chancery Court to compel Bank One to honor the exercise based on misrepresentation or equitable fraud. Initially, the trial court granted summary judgment to Bank One. On appeal to the Delaware Supreme Court, the case was reversed and remanded for a hearing on the issues. On remand, the trial court determined that misrepresentations were probably made, and that Vague could have reasonably relied on at least some of them. However, it concluded that Vague's claim was undermined by the fact that two statements were sent to him before August 2000 that accurately showed the expiration date. Vague forwarded those statements, unopened, to his accountant and thus was unaware of the problem until it came to his attention in the context of his personal financial matters.

Held: On rehearing, judgment entered for Bank One. Although Vague earned and should have been entitled to exercise the options, he would in all likelihood have done so timely if he had read the accurate statements that were sent to him by Bank One prior to the expiration date. The fact that he did not does not save his misrepresentation claim.

No right to additional vesting when misunderstanding could have been corrected by reading plan document

In *Butvin v. Doubleclick, Inc.*, 2001 WL 22812 (S.D.N.Y. Mar. 7, 2001) (unpublished), plaintiff Butvin was employed by Doubleclick for one year, terminating seven months before the company's IPO. On hire he was granted an option that vested over four years under the terms of the agreement and the option plan. His option agreement set out a three-month post-termination exercise period so long as termination was "without good reason." Butvin claimed he believed this language meant all of his options would vest and become exercisable on his termination. He further claimed that as of the date of exercise, he had been under the impression from discussions with company representatives that (notwithstanding the references to the plan in the option agreement) no plan document actually existed. Doubleclick permitted him to exercise as to 25% of the grant only, and Butvin sued to compel exercise of the full grant based on fraud.

Held: Summary judgment for defendant Doubleclick. Butvin had signed an agreement that specifically referenced the plan, and had he reviewed the plan, he would have understood the vesting provisions. The trial court concluded that even if it were true that Doubleclick employees had falsely represented that there was no plan, Butvin was still required to investigate the terms in his option agreement before he signed that agreement.

See also *First Marblehead Corp. v. House,* discussed above (sophisticated plaintiff could not claim that he did not know he should read his option grants before termination); *Sheils v. Pfizer Inc.,* 156 Fed. App'x. 446 (3rd Cir. 2005) (unpublished) (plaintiff's claim that he did not know that he was required to exercise options through a captive broker was irrelevant in light of his failure in any event to deliver an exercise notice within three months after termination); *Lin v. Qualcomm Inc.* (D036196, Cal. Ct. App. Feb. 13, 2002) (unpublished) (dismissing plaintiff's claim that, after a cashless exercise, he did not realize his remaining option shares were still subject to the post-termination exercise period); *Lynch v. Nortel Networks Corp.,* 2002 Mass. Super. LEXIS 449 (Mass. Super. Ct. Nov. 4, 2002) (employee cannot rely on mistake about expiration dates received from broker over phone when he could have simply looked at his own stock option agreements for correct information).

4. Miscellaneous Contract Issues

Generally, oral promises to grant options are unenforceable

As a rule, an oral promise to grant equity that is never reduced to writing will not to be an enforceable contract. *See, e.g., Braun v. CMGI,* 64 Fed. App'x. 301 (2d Cir. 2003) (unpublished) (applying New York law); *Ingram v. Rencor Controls Inc.,* No. 02-58-P-C (D. Me. Apr. 11, 2003) (applying Maine law); *Romaine v. Colonial Tanning Corp.,* 301 A.D. 2d 732 (N.Y. App. Div. Jan. 2, 2003) (applying New York law); *Rodriguez v. Vision Corr. Group, Inc.,* 260 Ga. App. 478 (Mar. 20, 2003) (applying Georgia law); *Sullivan v. Sovereign Bancorp, Inc.,* 2002 U.S. App. LEXIS 8311 (3d. Cir. 2002) (applying Pennsylvania law); *Richards v. Jain,* 168 F. Supp. 2d 1195 (W.D. Wash. 2001) (applying Washington law). *Black v. Hoffman,* No. 00-1797 (4th Cir. Apr. 13, 2001) (unpublished). *See also*

Grimes v. Alteon, Inc., 804 A.2d 256 (Del. July 19, 2002) (oral promise to purchase stock unenforceable under Delaware law); *Alexander v. Codemasters Group Ltd.*, 104 Cal. App. 4th 129 (Cal. Ct. App. 2002) (oral promise regarding vesting). Moreover, a claim that certain oral promises were not incorporated into the final written option agreement, or that the agreement was orally modified contrary to its terms, is as unlikely to succeed in an equity claim as it is in any other contract claim. *See, e.g., Syverson v. FirePond Inc.*, 383 F.3d 745 (8th Cir. 2004).

But a written promise to grant equity rights (particularly phantom stock) may be enforceable even if specific grants were never made

See, e.g., Hopmayer v. Aladdin Indus., LLC, No. M2003-01583-COA-R3-DV (Tenn. Ct. App. June 9, 2004) (employment offer letter promising phantom stock was sufficient grounds to establish mutually agreed contract); *Montemayor v. Jacor Communications, Inc.*, 64 P.3d 916 (Colo. Ct. App. Oct. 24, 2002), *cert. denied* 2003 Colo. LEXIS 147 (Feb. 24, 2003) (failure to make stock option grant specifically set out in employment agreement constitutes breach of contract); *Moulos v. Lucent Technologies Inc.*, No. 02 C 550 (N.D. Ill. Nov. 15, 2002) (statements made in employee handbook regarding phantom stock sufficiently specific to be enforced under Delaware law). *See also DiLorenzo v. Valve & Primer Corp.*, 779 N.E.2d 280 (Ill. App. Ct. Sept. 6, 2002), *vacated and remanded* 785 N.E.2d 860 (Ill. Apr. 2, 2003), *remanded* 2003 Ill. App. LEXIS 710 (Ill. App. Ct. June 6, 2003) (board minutes may, if authentic, prove existence of stock option agreement).

You take your risks with equity compensation

There are no guarantees, and optionees are expected to understand that an equity grant may not produce results as good as straight cash compensation. *See, e.g., Martino-Catt v. E.I. Dupont Nemours and Co.*, 317 F. Supp. 2d 914 (S.D. Iowa Apr. 29, 2004) (motion for summary judgment decided in favor of company when former employee voluntarily waived rights in a change in control plan in exchange for stock options and then sued when stock price declined); *Bors v. Duberstein*, No. 03 C

4636 (N.D. Ill. July 1, 2004) (executives did not have an obligation to tell an employee about the company's future outlook when it persuaded her to trade her phantom stock plan for restricted stock, even though the company later went bankrupt).

CHAPTER 2

Equity Issues Related to Employment Disputes

Contents

1. **Recent Cases on the Effects of Termination** 20
   Right of repurchase for unvested shares on termination valid 20
   Post-termination exercise period cannot begin until employee
   knows he is terminated 21

2. **Options as Wages** 22
   Stock options not wages under Maryland law 22
   Idaho court must rule on whether options are wages 23
   Inclusion of stock option gains for purposes of calculating
   retirement plan benefits is based on past practice 24

3. **Noncompete Agreements and Stock Option Forfeitures** 25
   Choice of law on noncompetes governs enforceability of stock
   option forfeiture clause 25
   Strange goings-on in Texas: Unenforceable noncompete,
   enforceable forfeiture 26
   Forfeiture clauses: A note of caution to companies that do business
   in California 27

4. **Calculating Damages When the Breach of an Equity Agreement
   Is Related to Termination** 29
   Value of stock option damages measured as of date option
   agreement breached 30
   Value of stock option damages measured as of date of wrongful
   termination 30

When an employee leaves employment for a reason other than death or disability, a number of equity-related issues can arise that lead to a dispute.

In recent years, allegations of unfair treatment with respect to options have increasingly formed the basis for claims in wrongful termination litigation. Litigation particularly arises with respect to disputes over vesting and exercise rights on termination. Such claims are governed by state law and generally turn on contract construction. Wrongful termination and noncompete clauses that implicate equity grants are particularly tricky. For example, a company may seek to use equity as a form of severance, either by accelerating vesting or by extending exercise terms. At the other end of the spectrum, a company may attempt to create an equity-based noncompete agreement by including (and enforcing) forfeiture clauses in all option grants. Employees who sue to retain options on the basis of wrongful termination have had mixed success in the cases reported below, largely because state law varies as to whether terminations without good cause vitiate compensation promises.

1. Recent Cases on the Effects of Termination

In the context of a claim of wrongful termination, everything—including vested and unvested stock options—is up for grabs. Plaintiffs should expect to fail if they argue that a termination is wrongful merely because it prevents continued stock vesting. However, facts that show an actual attempt to terminate an employee in such a way as to deprive him or her of vested rights will garner judicial sympathy.

Right of repurchase for unvested shares on termination valid

In *Harrison v. NetCentric Corp.,* 433 Mass. 465 (2001), plaintiff Harrison was 45% vested in his restricted stock at the time of his termination. Pursuant to Harrison's restricted stock agreement, the company had a right to repurchase unvested shares at their original purchase price within 90 days of his employment termination. In an action for wrongful termination and breach of implied covenant of fair dealing, Harrison claimed (among other things) that the company fired him to prevent him from continuing to vest in the shares. In addition, he maintained that the stock was granted for past services and therefore should have been fully vested as of his termination date.

Held: On appeal to the Massachusetts Supreme Court, summary judgment upheld in favor of defendant NetCentric. Harrison had a normal grant with normal vesting, 55% of which had not yet been earned. As an at-will employee, he could be fired without cause under Massachusetts law. Without more, Netcentric had no obligation to vest Harrison's stock or pay more than the contractually provided repurchase price.

See also *Salsgiver v. America Online, Inc.*, 147 F. Supp. 2d 1022 (C.D. Col. 2000) aff'd (9th Cir. 2002) (unpublished) (mere fact that options vest as a result of continuing service does not provide protection against termination for an at-will employee in California); *Irvine v. Capstone Turbine Corp.*, 2002 Cal. App. Unpub. LEXIS 3603 (Feb. 27, 2002) (stock option agreement does not create right to continuing employment for at-will employee). *Cf. Nofs v. Gemini Network, Inc.*, 2003 Conn. Super. LEXIS 316 (Conn. Super. Ct. Feb. 4, 2003) (company must pay value of vested options when termination of employee was for purpose of avoiding payment of benefits); *Scully v. US Watts, Inc.*, 238 F.3d 497 (3d Cir. 2001) (company must permit post-termination exercise when its breach of contract prevented options from vesting).

Post-termination exercise period cannot begin until employee knows he is terminated

In *Pollen v. Aware, Inc.*, 53 Mass. App. Ct. 823 (Mass. Ct. App. 2002), plaintiff Pollen was a Harvard student who worked part-time for Aware in the 1980s, then full-time, and then went to graduate school on a leave of absence, returning to Aware intermittently on a consulting basis. The company kept him on as a regular employee, however, with an extended leave of absence. In 1994, he decided to return to full-time graduate work, but, to maintain his leave-of-absence status at Aware, he did some unpaid work. He received a letter confirming that this work would maintain that status. In 1996, Aware had its IPO, and Pollen tried to exercise stock options he had been granted as an employee. The company returned the check, saying that his employment had been terminated, so he could not, under terms of the options agreement, exercise the awards. The company contended that it had orally notified Pollen that his leave of absence had ended and that he was terminated; Pollen denied having received such notice. There was no written record of the notice.

Held: Summary judgment (on this claim) affirmed for plaintiff. The court held that the company had the obligation to inform Pollen that he had been terminated in order to give him the opportunity to exercise his options. Note that this meant that Pollen was awarded the value of options as of the date of the IPO, not as of the date (two years earlier) the company claimed that the termination had occurred.

2. Options as Wages

The question of whether income derived from stock options may be classified as "wages" for labor law purposes continues to produce lawsuits nationwide. Similar issues arise in the context of state unemployment and workers' compensation laws. Because state law is the final arbiter on this matter, there is no uniformity among the different jurisdictions. Problems particularly arise when the federal courts must interpret state law. Where permitted by state law, the federal court will sometimes choose to certify the question to the highest state court for a determination (see, for example, *Paolini v. Albertson's, Inc.*, discussed below). In others, the federal court has chosen to apply state law, sometimes with dubious results (for example, in *IBM v. Bajorek*, where a panel of the same court arguably misapplied California law). It is always important to remember that an interpretation of state law by a federal appellate court applies only to the federal courts in that specific circuit; it is not binding on the state courts or on any other federal courts.

Stock options not wages under Maryland law

In *Varghese v. Honeywell International Inc.*, 424 F.3d 511 (4th Cir. 2005), plaintiff Varghese worked for Honeywell for 16 years before taking a leave of absence to pursue graduate studies, and vested in 4,800 options during that time. Varghese requested reinstatement at Honeywell in May 1999 but was told that his job was no longer available. After waiting until October, Varghese wrote to say he was seeking termination and severance pay. He attempted to exercise his options in October and November, but the company refused to permit him to do so, saying that it had backdated his termination to May and that the plan only allowed him three months to exercise the options after termination. Varghese sued Honeywell on a violation of the Maryland Wage Payment & Collection Law (MWP&CL), and the jury awarded him $337,000 in enhanced damages under that law.

Held: Reversed on appeal to the U.S. Court of Appeals for the Fourth Circuit. The appellate court construed the MWP&CL in such a way as to exclude options from the definition of "wages." After reviewing Maryland case law, the court concluded that remuneration must be guaranteed in order to be a "wage" for these purposes and that options are discretionary payments only.

See also *Hmelyar v. Phoenix Controls,* 2003 WL 21436530 (Ill. Ct. App. June 17, 2003) (options not wages for purposes of Illinois Unemployment Insurance Act); *Scott v. Workers' Comp. Appeal Bd.,* 814 A.2d 298 (Pa. Comm. Ct. Jan. 3, 2003) (options not wages for purposes of Pennsylvania workers' compensation claims).

But cf. *Scully v. US Watts, Inc.,* 238 F.3d 497 (3d Cir. 2001) (stock options wages for purposes of Pennsylvania Wage Payment and Collection Law); *Galdieri v. Monsanto Co.,* 245 F. Supp. 2d 636 (E.D. Pa. 2002) (same); *Montemayor v. Jacor Communications, Inc.,* 64 P.3d 916 (Colo. Ct. App. Oct. 24, 2002), *cert. denied* 2003 Colo. LEXIS 147 (Feb. 24, 2003) (stock options wages for purposes of Colorado Wage Claims Act).

Idaho court must rule on whether options are wages

In *Paolini v. Albertson's Inc.,* 418 F.3d 1023 (9th Cir. 2005), plaintiff Paolini was a 17-year executive at Albertson's resident in Idaho. In 2001, he attempted to exercise his options because he believed there had been a change in control at the company (a matter in dispute but not relevant to the court's findings). Paolini believed that the change in control triggered plan provisions for accelerated vesting of his remaining options. He subsequently left the company, also for reasons in dispute. The company claimed he quit; he claimed he was fired for trying to exercise his options. The trial court awarded summary judgment to the company, and Paolini appealed to the U.S. Court of Appeals for the Ninth Circuit.

Held: Submission vacated and questions certified to the Idaho Supreme Court for a determination regarding whether options are wages under Idaho law. The appellate court concluded that there was evidence that Paolini was fired because of his effort to exercise the options and that the ultimate decision will turn on whether options are wages under Idaho law, a matter on which Idaho has no clear legal precedent. In this case, the plan's administrator and some of the material describing the plan called options "compensation," although this in itself is not enough to establish that they are compensation for wage purposes. Further, assuming that options are wages, the Idaho Supreme Court must also decide whether Paolini's firing was a public-policy violation of Idaho's at-will employment laws. If so, then Paolini can proceed in an action based on Idaho employment law; if not, the case should be dismissed.

See also Brown v. Nortel Networks, 2002 Mass. Super. LEXIS 159 (2002) (denying motion for summary judgment on whether options are wages under the Massachusetts wage act because no clear state precedent). *But see IBM v. Bajorek*, discussed below, where a different panel of the Ninth Circuit held that it could decide—without credible reference to California precedent—that options are not wages for purposes of California labor law. This highly questionable result directly conflicts with the analogous analysis in *Paolini*.

Inclusion of stock option gains for purposes of calculating retirement plan benefits is based on past practice

In *Adams v. Louisiana-Pacific Corp.*, 284 F. Supp. 2d 311 (W.D.N.C. 2003), the plaintiff was an employee of ABT Building Products, which had a SERP and a stock option plan for its top executives. In 1999, ABT was merged into Louisiana-Pacific. Adams cashed out his options in ABT at the time. The new SERP committee at Louisiana-Pacific determined that notwithstanding the plan and past practice of ABT, stock option gains going forward would not be included in compensation for purposes the SERP.

Held: Judgment for plaintiff. The exclusion was unreasonable. Consistent with prior administrative practice, stock option gains must be considered as "compensation" rather than "fringe benefits" for purposes of calculating plan benefits.

Scipio v. United National Bankshares, 84 F. Supp. 2d 411 (N.D. W. Va. 2003), presents the opposite facts: defendant United National Bankshares, Inc. had consistently *excluded* option gains from the definition of "earnings" when calculating retirement benefits. Plaintiff argued that because the term was undefined in the plan, stock options should be included (which would have resulted in $50,000 more per year in retirement benefits than he made when working). *Held: Judgment for defendant.*

3. Noncompete Agreements and Stock Option Forfeitures

Another unsettled area of the law involves using stock option forfeitures as a way of enforcing post-employment noncompete agreements. The enforceability of such agreements, and thus the validity of requiring forfeiture, is—like the classification of options as wages—entirely a matter of state law. Where state law eschews noncompetes as a matter of public policy (for example, in California), the ability to require stock option forfeitures will be highly constrained. Even where noncompetes are permitted, they will generally be subject to state law limitations and restrictions as to reasonableness and scope. Accordingly, no analysis of an action related to stock option forfeiture on violation of a noncompete may proceed without a careful review of the law governing restraint on trade in the employee's state.

Choice of law on noncompetes governs enforceability of stock option forfeiture clause

In *Lucente v. International Business Machines Corp.*, 117 F. Supp. 2d 336 (S.D.N.Y. 2000), *rev'd and remanded,* 310 F.3d 243 (2d Cir. 2002); *consent settlement decree entered* Oct. 2003, IBM sued former executive Edward Lucente, claiming he violated his noncompete agreement. IBM is well known for its policy of litigating to enforce stock option forfeiture by former employees who IBM claims have violated their noncompete agreements. In *Lucente*, a case that was aggressively litigated over a four-year period (ending with the entry of a consent settlement decree in October 2003), former IBM executive Lucente left IBM in 1991 after being told "it would be in the best interests of Lucente and IBM if he sought employment elsewhere." In anticipation of this, Lucente took a job with Northern Telecom, which IBM agreed would not violate his noncompete agreement. He received a severance package that included cash and also continued to have rights to certain unexpired restricted stock and option grants. Two years later, Lucente joined Digital Equipment, a company that IBM considers to be a competitor. IBM notified Lucente that it was canceling his remaining stock options and restricted stock. Lucente sued for breach of contract; IBM countersued for return of the severance pay.

The trial court held for Lucente based on the unreasonableness of the forfeiture clause.

Held: On appeal to the U.S. Court of Appeals for the Second Circuit, reversed and remanded to district court. Applying New York law, the appellate court held that the enforceability of the forfeiture clause hinged on whether the competing employee had left voluntarily or had been terminated by IBM (the "employee choice doctrine"). If the employee was found to have left voluntarily, New York law would apply to enforce the clause regardless of whether the noncompete provision was reasonable. On remand, Lucente requested that IBM disclose information on how it interpreted its noncompete agreements with former employees in other situations, and IBM resisted the discovery, arguing that a different standard should be applied to stock forfeitures than to standard noncompetes. The district court disagreed and ordered discovery in May 2003. As noted above, the case settled shortly thereafter, so the question of reasonableness was never resolved.

See also *Keener v. Convergys Corp.*, 342 F.3d 1264 (11th Cir. 2003) (broad noncompete clause entered into under Ohio law unenforceable in Georgia and thus stock option forfeiture invalid); *Pfizer Inc. v. Gilman*, 2002 U.S. Dist. LEXIS 2174 (S.D.N.Y. Feb. 13, 2002) (forfeiture of options valid under New York law). *But see Tatom v. Ameritech Corp.*, 305 F.3d 737 (7th Cir. 2002) (noncompete requiring forfeiture of options not a restraint on trade for purposes of Illinois law).

Strange goings-on in Texas: Unenforceable noncompete, enforceable forfeiture

In the strange case of *Olander v. Compass Bank*, 363 F.3d 560 (5th Cir. 2004), plaintiff Olander was barred by a broad noncompete from associating with interests contrary to his employer, Compass Bank. However, the contract also stated that if the clause were ruled invalid or unenforceable, then the clawback would kick in: i.e., Compass would be entitled to claim any profits from option exercises, plus any common stock held by Olander. Olander left Compass Bank to work for another bank in 2001, violating the terms of the agreement, but he won a declaratory judgment from the trial court that the noncompete was unenforceable. Compass then filed an action for restoration of profits under the clawback, which it lost at the trial level.

Held: On appeal to the U.S. Court of Appeals for the Fifth Circuit, both for and against plaintiff. The appellate court held that (1) the noncompete was unenforceable and (2) because the noncompete was unenforceable, a "clawback provision" in the same contract requiring the executive to repay profits earned from exercising options was valid. Calling Olander's victory "pyrrhic," the court noted that the noncompete was unenforceable because the options were valuable only while Olander remained an employee of Compass (an "illusory" promise because Compass could terminate him at will). Nonetheless, the agreement clearly provided that if Olander won on the noncompete issue, he would lose on the option issue.

But see Dell Computer Corp. v. Rodriguez, 2004 U.S. App. LEXIS 23393 (5th Cir. Nov. 8, 2004) (applying Texas law with respect to a clawback provision that would have required a former Dell executive to pay back gains realized under stock option and stock purchase agreements).

Forfeiture clauses: A note of caution to companies that do business in California

As discussed above, forfeiture clauses have been used successfully by large companies (most notably, IBM) to force former employees to disgorge option profits in the event a noncompete is violated. Whether or not such clauses are advisable, they are clearly enforceable in many, if not most, states.

Companies that employ California residents, however, need to be aware that it is generally illegal under California Business and Professions Code Section 16600 to require an employee to agree to a post-employment restraint on trade. Although in *IBM v. Bajorek,* 191 F.3d 1033 (9th Cir. 1999) the U.S. Court of Appeals for the Ninth Circuit upheld IBM's forfeiture clause as applied to a California resident, many California lawyers believe that the federal panel substantially misinterpreted California law in coming to its decision. The facts of the case are that the former employee, Dr. Bajorek, signed a boilerplate employment agreement with IBM that included (1) a forfeiture provision providing for disgorgement of any profits made on the exercise of options if Bajorek joined a competitor within six months of leaving IBM and (2) a choice-of-law provision stipulating that New York law would apply in interpreting the agreement. Dr. Bajorek worked and lived entirely in California. Before terminating employment with IBM, he exercised his vested options and realized a spread of approximately $900,000. After leaving, he joined a company that IBM considered to be a competitor. IBM sued Bajorek for breach of contract and lost at the district court level. The U.S. District Court found in favor of Bajorek, holding that the IBM noncompete provision violated California's strong public policies against restraint of trade (and in favor of protecting employee wages). On appeal, a panel of the Ninth Circuit reversed and remanded for judgment under New York law, which has no such protective policies.

A careful reading of the decision reveals that the Ninth Circuit made at least two serious errors. First, it ignored Bajorek's argument that the governing law provision was non-negotiable boilerplate and assumed that he willingly agreed to subject himself to New York law. More importantly for our purposes, the Ninth Circuit completely misunderstood the nature of the amounts realized on exercise of the stock option. In his strangely reasoned opinion, Judge Andrew J. Kleinfeld, writing for the panel, made the following observation:

> The [California Labor Law] statute does not apply because its words read literally and in light of its purposes do not apply—stock options are not "wages." Wages are defined by the statute as "all amounts for labor performed by employees of every description, whether the amount is fixed or ascertained by the standard of time, task, piece, commission basis or another method of calculation." Stock options are not "amounts." They are not money at all. They are contractual rights to buy shares of stock. The purposes of . . . protecting employee's reliance interests in their expected wages do not apply to stock options.

From there, the opinion goes on to state that the options cannot be treated as wages because "the value that Dr. Bajorek obtained from them depended largely on the vagaries of the stock market valuations on those dates." Because the ultimate value of the option is not fixed at time of grant, the employee may not claim that he has earned it. Despite the huge weight of tax, accounting, securities, and California employment law to the contrary on this issue, Judge Kleinfeld cites no authorities for his conclusion that the proceeds from Bajorek's fully vested options did not constitute wages in California.

Since *IBM v. Bajorek*, California state courts have expressed disapproval of the Ninth Circuit's analysis of the California policy and statutory provision at issue. In *Walia v. Aetna*, 93 Cal. App. 4th 1213 (Cal. Ct. App. 2001), the First District Court of Appeal for California was presented with a challenge to a noncompete clause similar in scope to that in *Bajorek*. In finding for the employee, the court rejected Aetna's argument that the reasoning in *Bajorek* now authorizes the use of broad noncompete clauses in California. Instead, the opinion specifically states that *"IBM,* in fact, *is* contrary to California law because it is contradicted by [previous California Supreme Court cases]" (emphasis in original).

Potential litigants should be aware that the conflict between *Walia* and *Bajorek* highlights an ongoing grey area with respect to the status of option forfeitures under California employment law. *Walia* was certified to the California Supreme Court but ultimately settled. Since *Walia,* at least one California court has cited *Bajorek* as for the proposition that stock options are not wages in California. *See Hanig v. Qualcomm, Inc.*, No. D038513 (Cal. Ct. App. Dec. 6, 2002) (unpublished). However, it is always important to remember that a federal appellate court's interpretation of state law is binding only on the federal courts in the same circuit; it has no impact on the state courts' interpretation of their own state law. It remains to be seen where the California courts will end up on this issue.

4. Calculating Damages When the Breach of an Equity Agreement Is Related to Termination

Once a former employee establishes that the company has breached its agreement to provide equity compensation, the court (and/or jury) is confronted with the difficult task of placing an economic value on the employee's equity rights. The initial hurdle is timing: does valuation occur on the date of termination, on the date the optionee claims he or she would have exercised if not prevented by the company, or on some other date entirely? Once a date for valuation is established, how is it achieved? Should price averaging be applied, or perhaps a market discount? What about lost opportunity cost? As one might expect, there is no uniform answer, and the courts continue can be expected to respond to arguments about appropriate methodology for each set of facts.

Value of stock option damages measured as of date option agreement breached

In *Miga v. Jensen*, 96 S.W.3d 207 (Tex. Oct. 31, 2002), *rehearing denied* (Feb. 27, 2003), plaintiff Miga was hired to work for a newly formed telecommunications company in 1990. In 1992, the owner of the company (Jensen) made an investment in another company, Pacific Gateway Exchange (PGE), and orally promised Miga the right to receive 4.8% of Jensen's total shares in PGE. Miga resigned in 1994 and signed a termination agreement. At the time of termination, Jensen assured Miga that he would still be able to purchase stock in PGE. Ultimately, he failed to make good on his assurances, and Miga sued for the promised 4.8%. Jensen contended Miga's option expired at the time of his termination of employment. PGE's stock subsequently split 940 to 1, the company went public, and the shares rose from $12 to $36 in the next two years.

At trial, the jury awarded Miga $18.8 million, including $1.03 million for breach of contract and $17.8 million for "lost profits" (the value of the underlying stock as of the trial date), plus pre-judgment interest. Jensen appealed the "lost profits" part of the award, saying that the damages should have been measured as of the date the agreement was violated. The appellate court struck $1 million as double recovery but affirmed the "lost profits" calculation.

Held: Reversed and remanded by Texas Supreme Court on the issue of damages. Under Texas law, contract damages are measured as of date of breach rather than value as of date of trial. There was no certainty at the time of breach that the stock would appreciate, so the correct measure of damages was $1 million (the difference between strike price and fair market value at time of proposed exercise), plus interest.

See also Edwards v. Schrader-Bridgeport International, Inc., 205 F. Supp. 2d 3 (N.D.N.Y. 2002) (company required to pay interest on liquidated value of vested options from date it refused to permit plaintiff to exercise).

Value of stock option damages measured as of date of wrongful termination

In *Scully v. US Watts, Inc.*, 238 F.3d 497 (3d Cir. 2001), plaintiff Scully was wrongfully terminated before the end of his employment agreement, resulting in the unilateral cancellation of all of his options before exercise.

At the time of his termination, the options were valued at $531,000. Six months later, when the options would have vested had he not been fired, they would have been worth $1,078,000. At trial, the U.S. District Court for the Eastern District of Pennsylvania concluded that the correct measurement date was the date of termination. In doing so, it rejected the plaintiff's theory that the date should be set at the time all restrictions would have lifted (i.e., vesting) as well as the defendant's theory that the unexercised shares should be valued using a 30% marketability discount.

Held: Affirmed on this issue by the U.S. Court of Appeals for the Third Circuit. This case includes a detailed discussion of basic contract law damage theories. The court noted that computing stock option damages is a difficult task and that there is no one method that will apply in every instance. The goal is to put the plaintiff in the position he or she would have been in at the time of the breach had the plaintiff received the benefit of his or her bargain.

But cf. Bedrosian v. Tenet Healthcare Corp., B166742 (Cal. Ct. App. Oct. 28, 2003), *modified* November 25, 2003, *cert. denied* S121071 (Cal. Feb. 18, 2004) (unpublished) ($148 million damage award based on valuing option rights at highest market price optionee could have achieved had he timely exercised and held his stock through the top trading date).

CHAPTER 3

TREATMENT OF EQUITY IN CORPORATE TRANSACTIONS

Contents

1. Change-in-Control Date Issues 34
   Acceleration of vesting triggered only if merger is actually completed 34
   Employees who terminate after merger agreement signed but before stockholder approval obtained are not entitled to acceleration 34
   Sale of bankrupt company's assets triggers change in control 35
2. Exercise After Spin-Off or Divestiture 36
   Sale of subsidiary constitutes a termination of employment for purposes of stock option plan 36

In the best of all worlds, every equity incentive plan would include a specific provision addressing what happens to outstanding employee rights at the time of a merger, acquisition, or other corporate transaction. Many plans and agreements, however, are ambiguous on how to treat such matters or fail to address them at all. Confusion as to what rules apply often leads to litigation, particularly when a corporate transaction is the trigger for equity rights to be accelerated. On what date, for example, does a change in control occur—at the time a merger agreement is signed, or only on closing? What happens if an optionee's termination of employment occurs between the two dates? Does a spin-off of a subsidiary act to terminate its employees' employment at the former parent for purposes of a stock option plan if the plan does not specifically contemplate such treatment? In the last few years, each of these questions has been considered by the courts.

1. Change-in-Control Date Issues

A surprising number of cases involve arguments over when and if a "change in control" or other corporate transaction actually occurred. In general, courts have concluded that a transaction does not occur until it actually closes. Plaintiffs have not had much luck arguing that imprecise language in an agreement (e.g., pegging acceleration to the execution date of a merger agreement rather than to the closing date of the deal) will support a trigger event even when the deal falls through.

Acceleration of vesting triggered only if merger is actually completed

In *Bohan v. Honeywell International Inc.*, 366 F.3d 606 (8th Cir. 2004), the plaintiffs argued they were entitled to full acceleration of vesting of their stock options as of the date that shareholders of Honeywell and General Electric had approved a merger agreement. Shareholder approval was obtained in January 2002, but the merger fell through in July when European regulators blocked it. The employees contended that, under the terms of the plan, shareholder approval was sufficient to trigger acceleration. At trial, the district court determined that the plan required that a merger had to be "completed"; i.e., approval was not enough. In fact, the plan specifically stated that "the Company will no longer survive as an independent publicly held corporation" and provided that option vesting would accelerate "on or following . . . a merger."

Held: Affirmed by U.S. Circuit Court for the Eighth Circuit, for defendant. The plan language requiring shareholder approval cannot be read separately from the language specifying that acceleration would occur only on a merger.

See also *Dubbs v. Net Value Holdings*, 2003 Cal. App. Unpub. LEXIS 999 (Jan. 30, 2003) (unpublished) (options promised contingent on merger need not be granted when closing never occurred).

Employees who terminate after merger agreement signed but before stockholder approval obtained are not entitled to acceleration

In *AirTouch Communications Inc. v. Nott-Kilfoil*, 2002 Cal. App. Unpub. LEXIS 11621 (Cal. Ct. App. Dec. 16, 2002) (unpublished) and *Pasquel v. AirTouch Communications, Inc.*, 2002 Cal. App. Unpub. LEXIS 11623 (Cal. Ct. App. Dec. 16, 2002) (unpublished), plaintiffs Nott-Kilfoil and Pasquel each held options under the AirTouch Communications Long Term Stock Incentive Plan, which provided that unvested options would accelerate on a change in control. Change in control was defined, among other things, to occur when the "stockholders of the Company approve a merger or consolidation."

On January 15, 1999, the board of directors of AirTouch entered into a merger agreement with Vodaphone. Stockholder approval (and closing) did not occur for almost six months. Plaintiff and Pasquel each terminated their employment after January 15, 1999, but before stockholder approval was obtained. The plaintiffs argued that, for purposes of the acceleration clause, "change in control" should be deemed to have occurred at the merger agreement was executed. In particular, Nott-Kilfoil argued that her option agreement provided for acceleration when the company became "*subject* to a change in control" rather than just at the time the definition of "change in control" was met (i.e., by obtaining stockholder approval). The trial court found this argument unpersuasive and held that acceleration could not occur until the date of stockholder approval.

Held: On appeal, trial court judgment in favor of AirTouch affirmed. The definition of change in control specifically requires stockholder approval for completion. The company was under no obligation to accelerate vesting for employees who terminated before such completion.

See also *Bau v. Actamed Corporation*, 562 S.E. 2d 734 (Ga. Ct. App. 2002), *cert. denied*, 123 S. Ct. 1487 (2003) (same); *Elgaway v. Watkins-Johnson Company* (HO22472, Cal. Ct. App.-6th Dist. June 5, 2002) (same). *Cf. Hurd v. Spine-Tech, Inc.*, 2002 Minn. App. LEXIS 1249 (Minn. Ct. App. Nov. 12, 2002) (no right to acceleration when change in control occurs during post-termination exercise period).

Sale of bankrupt company's assets triggers change in control

In *Fix v. Quantum Industrial Partners LDC*, 374 F.3d 549 (7th Cir. 2004), plaintiff Fix was hired by Quantum in 2000 as a turnaround specialist under an employment agreement that, among other things, provided that Fix would receive $5 million less the value of his stock options upon a change in control in Quantum's controlled subsidiary, OMC. For these purposes, change in control was defined to include a "sale of all or substantially all the assets of OMC." The definition did not contain a bankruptcy exception. OMC filed for bankruptcy in December 2000, and after Fix arranged for the sale of its assets, Quantum fired him and refused to honor the contract.

Quantum argued Fix was due compensation only if he created value at OMC by helping the company grow. However, the trial court held that under Delaware law, Fix's contract unambiguously provided for the CIC payment on an asset sale. The court noted that the many lawyers and sophisticated investors who negotiated the employment contract could easily have excluded bankruptcy from the CIC definition if Quantum had intended that result, but they did not do so.

Held: Affirmed by the U.S. Court of Appeals for the Seventh Circuit.

See also Walden v. Affiliated Computer Services, Inc., 2002 Tex. App. LEXIS 6396 (Tex. App.-Houston, 14th Dist. Aug. 29, 2002); *withdrawn, substituted by* 97 S.W.3d 303 (Tex. App.-Houston, 14th Dist. Jan 16, 2003) (transfer of assets by reason of insolvency is change in control for purposes of stock option plan).

2. Exercise After Spin-Off or Divestiture

Sale of subsidiary constitutes a termination of employment for purposes of stock option plan

In *Monsanto Co. v. Boustany,* 73 S.W.3d 225 (Tex. 2002), the plaintiffs were employees of Fisher Controls International, a wholly owned subsidiary of Monsanto. In 1992, Monsanto sold Fisher to Emerson Electric. The Monsanto compensation committee specifically determined that, under the terms of the company's stock incentive plan, the sale of the subsidiary constituted a "termination of employment" from Monsanto for all of its employees, and accordingly, any options held by continuing Fisher employees would expire if not exercised within 90 days of the closing. However, as an accommodation to the employees and in view of the fact that many of the options were underwater, the committee extended the post-termination exercise period for an additional nine months.

By 1996, Monsanto stock was trading for two to four times what it was worth in the one-year extension period in 1992–1993. At that time, plaintiffs attempted to exercise their options in Monsanto, arguing that the compensation committee's interpretation of the "termination" was incorrect because their employment with Fisher had continued, even though Fisher was no longer a subsidiary of Monsanto. The trial court granted summary judgment to Monsanto. On appeal, the appellate court reversed and remanded, holding for the plaintiffs that no termination of employment had occurred under the plan.

Held: Reversed by Texas Supreme Court (remand on unrelated issues). The court held that the incentive plan and stock option certificates were unambiguous and that a "termination of employment" occurred within the meaning of those agreements.

See also *Falkowski v. Imation Corp.*, 132 Cal. App. 4th 499 (Cal. Ct. App. 2005) (same); *Morschbach v. Household Int'l, Inc.*, 2002 U.S. Dist. LEXIS 1874 (D. Del. Feb. 6, 2002) (same). *Cf. Schor v. FMS Financial Corp.*, 814 A2d 1108 (N.J. Super. Ct. App. Dec 30, 2002) (ambiguous definition of "corporation" must be read in context of entire transaction). We are aware of attempts by at least two other plaintiffs to assert that continuing employees of a subsidiary should be entitled to additional vesting in the former parent's options after a spin-off. So far, the argument (even when made on facts as strong as those in *Boustany*) has failed to survive summary judgment at the trial court level; at this point, employees would be wise to assume that it is not a winner.

CHAPTER 4

Choice of Law Issues

Contents

1. **Disputes Implicating International Issues** 40
   Choice of California law in stock option agreement governs notwithstanding employment agreement 40
   U.S. Seizure of Options Not Unlawful 41

2. **Federal/State Preemption Issues** 41
   Federal securities law preempts state fraud claims concerning option value..42
   Stock plan incentives may give rise to securities fraud 42
   Original filing under ERISA not fatal to phantom stock contract claims 43

3. **Stock Options in Bankruptcy Claims** 44
   Employee claim to payment under option agreement partially allowed as post-petition administrative priority of Chapter 11 bankruptcy estate 44
   Stock options partially exempt from Chapter 7 bankruptcy claims 45
   Unvested options subject to bankruptcy claims 45

4. **Miscellaneous** 46
   Insurance coverage..46
   Arbitration 46

Because equity compensation arrangements touch on so many substantive areas of the law, issues frequently arise as to which body of law governs in a dispute. As we note throughout this book, courts will look to state law to resolve the majority of contract and divorce disputes. However, choice of law may be complicated by international concerns, federal preemption principles, or bankruptcy issues. Moreover, the contract itself may impose arbitration or other forms of alternative dispute resolution that, when enforceable, will be determinative.

1. Disputes Implicating International Issues

Stock option agreements, like any contracts, may set out choice of law provisions that provide for jurisdiction outside of the United States. Moreover, international law principles will apply to stock option proceeds when (as in the *Paridissiotis* case described below) criminal acts are at issue.

Choice of California law in stock option agreement governs notwithstanding employment agreement

In *Oracle Corp. v. Falotti*, 319 F.3d 1106 (9th Cir. 2003), *cert. denied*, 540 U.S. 875 (2003), plaintiff Falotti was a senior vice-president of Oracle working in Switzerland, working pursuant to an employment agreement that was governed by Swiss law. At the time of his termination, his unvested options were cancelled. However, on the purported date of termination, plaintiff visited a Swiss doctor to be treated for depression. He then filed a wrongful termination action in the U.S. District Court for the Northern District of California, contending that he was terminated because of his illness. Swiss law prohibits terminating an employee because of illness and requires a two-month notice before termination. Plaintiff argued that under his employment contract, Oracle was prohibited from canceling his right to exercise options for another four months: a two-month recovery period plus the two-month statutory notice period. The additional four-month period would have resulted in his options being vested and exercisable prior to termination. The district court granted summary judgment in favor of Oracle, holding that although Swiss law governed the employment contract, the option agreement (which included a choice of law provision) was governed by California law.

Held: Summary judgment affirmed on appeal to the U.S. Court of Appeals for the Ninth Circuit. The stock option agreement, and not the employment agreement, governed Falotti's stock option vesting. Even if under Swiss law Falotti was entitled to a four-month notice period, there was no requirement for him to continue to be eligible for stock option vesting during that period. The court deferred to the stock option agreement's grant of exclusive authority to Oracle's compensation committee to determine when an employee ceased to be employed for purposes of the stock plan.

See also *Intershop Communications AG v. Superior Court*, 104 Cal. App. 4th 191 (Cal. App.-1st Dist. 2002) (forum selection clause in stock option agreement providing for jurisdiction and governing law in Germany is enforceable).

U.S. seizure of options not unlawful

In *Paradissiotis v. United States*, 49 Fed. Cl. 16 (2001), plaintiff Paradissiotis was a Cyprus citizen employed by Coastal Corporation, a Delaware company. In 1986, he became a director of one of its subsidiaries, Holborn Oil Trading. Holborn owned one-third of a Cypriot company, Holborn Investment Company Ltd. (HICL). HICL's majority owner as of 1990 was a company controlled by the Libyan government. In 1986, the U.S. froze the assets of the Libyan government and its agents. Paradissiotis was considered to be an agent of the Libyan government because of his connection to HICL. His assets in the U.S. were frozen, including his stock options in Coastal, which subsequently expired unexercised. Paradissiotis sued the United States under the theory that the asset freeze was an unlawful taking.

Held: Motion to dismiss granted in favor of defendant. The seizure was consistent with laws protecting U.S. national interests, and Paradissiotis' contractual interests were overridden by national security concerns. The U.S. is permitted to freeze assets of individuals deemed to be agents of the Libyan government, including stock options held by an employee.

2. Federal/State Preemption Issues

Equity compensation is necessarily subject to federal and state securities laws, which may preempt state laws when a lawsuit is pled properly (for example, in a class action). Another area of potential pre-emption arises from the Employee Retirement Income Security Act of 1974 (ERISA), although in general courts have concluded that the typical equity compensation plan, without more, is not an ERISA plan.

Federal securities law preempts state fraud claims concerning option value

In *Falkowski v. Imation Corp.*, 309 F.3d 1123 (9th Cir. 2002), *amended* 320 F.3d 905 (9th Cir. 2003), the plaintiffs were Cemax employees with stock options granted under the Cemax stock plan. Subsequently, Cemax merged with Imation, and Cemax shares were exchanged for Imation shares. One year later, Imation sold Cemax to Kodak. Imation notified employees that they had 30 days to exercise their vested options after the closing. Imation had just recently announced a $200 million earnings write-off, and its stock value declined sharply. Plaintiffs filed an action for fraud (misrepresentation of stock value) and breach of contract in state court. Imation successfully removed the case to federal court, arguing that claims under state law for fraud were preempted by the Securities Litigation Uniform Standards Act (SLUSA).

Held: Removal affirmed. Federal securities laws, in this case SLUSA, pre-empt state fraud claims relating to the sale of securities. Options fit squarely into SLUSA: "unlike stock bonus plans, stock options involve contracts to sell stock for money on a later date."

Note that the fraud claims did not survive removal. The contract claims were remanded to state court in *Falkowski v. Imation Corp.*, 132 Cal. App. 4th 499 (Cal. Ct. App. 2005) (cited above in the section on corporate transactions).

Stock plan incentives may give rise to securities fraud

In *No. 84 Employer-Teamster Joint Council Pension Trust Fund v. America West Holding Corp.*, 320 F.3d 920 (9th Cir. 2003), *rehearing en banc denied*, 2003 U.S. App., LEXIS 10783 (9th Cir. 2003), *cert. denied* (2003), the plaintiff, the Teamsters Union, alleged that members of America West Holdings Corporation management consistently distorted financial information to make it more likely they would receive stock options and other equity incentives. America West filed for bankruptcy in 1994 and subsequently reorganized under a new plan in which Continental Airlines and Texas Pacific Group held voting control of the company. During the ensuing years, maintenance problems led to FAA investigations and operational difficulties. The lawsuit alleged that the controlling shareholders used their influence over management to get them to report that the maintenance problems were being addressed. Share prices rose to an all-time high by 1998, when a lock-up period for the sale of stock by the controlling investors lapsed. In fact, during this time maintenance problems remained, and America West entered into a secret settlement with the FAA on resolving the problem. During 1998, key insiders sold their stock. Managers reporting the results were not among those making these unusual insider sales. However, these same managers were eligible for stock options and other equity incentives if the company met certain targets. Equity awards were made during the period in question. The day after Continental sold its stock, public reports indicated that America West faced sanctions for its maintenance failures and that labor unrest threatened to cause further problems. The stock price fell sharply thereafter. The district court granted summary judgment to Continental, concluding that the misstatements were immaterial because they did not lead, when revealed, to an immediate drop in share prices, which, in fact, fell gradually over the next several months.

Held: Reversed and remanded for rehearing by the Ninth Circuit. The high and unusual number of insider stock sales raised sufficient reason to argue that these incentives could cause insiders to pressure management to report misleading results. Moreover, the fact that managers could receive equity awards if targets were met encouraged them to distort their reports to investors.

See also *Kushner v. Beverly Enterprises*, 317 F.3d 820 (8th Cir. 2002), *rehearing en banc denied*, 2003 U.S. App. LEXIS 3630 (8th Cir. 2003) (fact that defendant's compensation, including stock options, depends on corporate value or earnings does not without more establish motive to fraudulently misrepresent corporate value or earnings); *Wilson v. Bernstock*, 195 F. Supp. 2d 619 (D.N.J. 2002) (same).

Original filing under ERISA not fatal to phantom stock contract claims

In *Emmenegger v. Bull Moose Tube Co.*, 324 F.3d 616 (8th Cir. 2003), the plaintiff executives brought a claim under ERISA based on their employer's failure to pay out phantom stock. The U.S. District Court for the Eastern District of Missouri awarded judgment to plaintiffs.

Held: Reversed and remanded. The U.S. Court of Appeals for the Eighth Circuit held that the phantom stock plan was not an ERISA plan, and therefore the district court did not have federal subject matter jurisdiction for its review. The case was remanded for consideration on state breach of contract claims. (Note that the trial court subsequently held for the executives under state law and assessed interest. Missouri law makes prejudgment interest payments mandatory under breach of contract cases, and the state 9% fixed rate, not the lower federal rate, applied because the judgment ultimately was under state law.)

Cf. Oatway v. American International Group, Inc., 2002 U.S. Dist. LEXIS 1771 (D. Del. 2002), *aff'd*, 325 F.3d 184 (3d Cir. 2003) (holding that stock incentive plan is not an ERISA plan); *Raskin v. CyNet, Inc.*, 131 F. Supp. 2d 906 (S.D. Tex. 2001) (same). *See also Miller v. PPG Industries*, 237 F. Supp. 2d 756 (W.D. Ky. 2002) (dispute regarding whether termination was for disability does not change stock option breach of contract claim into ERISA claim).

3. Stock Options in Bankruptcy Claims

Stock options (or their proceeds) are subject to the claims of the bankruptcy estate. The main issues concern (1) whether the options are the property of the estate and therefore available to satisfy creditors, and (2) whether the options are as a result of post-petition employment and therefore exempt from attachment by the court. As in all bankruptcy cases, the facts will determine what type of allocations are made between the debtor and the estate.

Employee claim to payment under option agreement partially allowed as post-petition administrative priority of Chapter 11 bankruptcy estate

In *In re Pre-Press Graphics Co.*, 287 B.R. 726 (N.D. Ill. Jan. 6, 2003), a former employee of the debtor sought payment of post-petition compensation obligations under his employment and stock option agreements. When the company filed a Chapter 11 bankruptcy petition, the employee was assured his employment would continue. However, after the estate filed a motion to reject his agreements, the employee resigned and brought a suit seeking the value of his contracts (including his option agreements) on the theory he was entitled to receive such payments as a post-petition priority expense of administration because the employer benefited from his post-petition efforts. The creditors' committee argued the obligation was a pre-petition unsecured claim because the original contract obligation arose before the filing.

Held: Bankruptcy court allowed partial claim. The employee is entitled to the amount of the benefit allocable to the "inducement" to continue employment after the petition was filed.

Stock options partially exempt from Chapter 7 bankruptcy claims

In *In re Wick*, 276 F.3rd 412 (8th Cir. 2002), the debtor, Wick, held stock options in her employer at the time of the bankruptcy filing, which options were subsequently cashed out. When the trustee asserted claims against the proceeds of the options, Wick argued the options were exempt under either of two theories: either because their market value at the time of the filing could not be determined or because of the federal bankruptcy "wild card" provisions that allow a formula-based minimum amount of assets to be exempted from claims. The Bankruptcy Court ruled that the options were only one-third vested when the bankruptcy petition was filed, so the estate's interest was limited to one-third of the overall value of the options, less any other exemption. Subsequent appreciation was allocated to post-petition services. The U.S. District Court for the District of Minnesota reversed, holding that the entire proceeds from the options were exempt.

Held: Reversed and remanded by the U.S. Court of Appeals for the Eighth Circuit. The original apportionment by the Bankruptcy Court was reinstated, with one-third of the appreciated value of the stock going to the estate, less any exemptions, and the balance going to the debtor.

Unvested options subject to bankruptcy claims

In *In re Denadai*, 259 B.R. 801 (2001), *aff'd, Denadai v Preferred Capital Markets Inc.* (D. Mass, No. 01-40073-WGY Nov. 13, 2001), at the time debtor Denadai filed his bankruptcy petition, he held unvested options in Ziff-Davis, Inc. Shortly after filing, Ziff-Davis was acquired by CNET, and all of Denadai's options vested as of the date of the acquisition. Denadai attempted to exclude the options from attachment by the bankruptcy court, arguing that although the options were granted pre-petition, they were "fruits of post-petition labor" because they had been unexercisable until after the acquisition. Citing *Allen v. Levey (In re Allen)* (226 B.R. 857, Bankr. N.D. Ill 1998), the Bankruptcy Court determined that the options were property of the estate because the debtor had a contractual interest in the property at the time of the bankruptcy. The fact that the options did not become exercisable until after the petition was filed did not make them valueless to the estate. *Allen* divided the options pro-rata on exercise based on the percentage that had vested as of the petition by a creditor. Thus, the only question here is how to divide the options on exercise. The court applied a formula based on the percentage of days worked before and after acceleration occurred.

Held: Affirmed by the U.S. District Court for the District of Massachusetts. The trustee was directed to liquidate the options and apply the formula to the proceeds

4. Miscellaneous

Insurance coverage

See TVN Entertainment Corp. v. General Star Indemnity Corporation, 2003 U.S. App. LEXIS 3976 (9th Cir. Mar. 4, 2003) (insurance contract provision excluding losses from "commissions, bonuses, profit sharing, or benefits pursuant to a contract of employment" upheld).

Arbitration

Brown v. Coleman Company, Inc. 220 F.3d 1180 (10th Cir. 2000) (equitable enforcement of stock options legitimate subject matter for arbitration); Adamany v. Superior Court of Los Angeles County, 2002 Cal. App. Unpub. LEXIS 6823 (July 25, 2002) (same).

CHAPTER 5

Allocation of Equity Rights Under Family Law

Contents

Arizona **49**
    Employer's intent a critical issue in dividing options 49
    Vested options count for child support 49

Arkansas **50**
    Income from future stock options includable in alimony settlement 50

California **50**
    Exercised stock options are includible in child support calculations 50
    Extra year added to time rule to account for vesting 51

Connecticut **51**
    Post-separation, pre-dissolution options are marital property 51
    Unvested options not marital assets 52

Florida **52**
    Stock options for future performance are not spouse's separate property 52

Maryland **53**
    Both vested and unvested options may be subject to division 53

Massachusetts **53**
    Unvested options are assets includible in marital estate 53

Minnesota 53
   Trial court has broad discretion to value options 53

Missouri 54
   Stock options granted the day after divorce becomes final are not subject to division in divorce settlement 54
   Options awarded before dissolution are marital property, even if unvested 54

New Hampshire 55
   Unvested options divided according to when they were earned 55

New Jersey 55
   Wife not entitled to half of options granted just before divorce 55
   Stock options granted after divorce excludable from child support calculation 56

North Carolina 56
   Court allows intrinsic value method for options in divorce case 56

Ohio 57
   Stock options granted during marriage are subject to division 57

Pennsylvania 57
   Parent's income includes unexercised vested options 57
   Unvested options are marital assets 57

Washington 58
   Stock option proceeds deposited in various investment accounts marital property 58
   Options are community property, including increase in share value post-exercise 59
   Options valued as of date of vesting 60

Divorce cases raise the difficult issue of how to allocate equity awards between former spouses. Vested awards generally are split along with the rest of the property, but unvested awards raise stickier issues. Most states have some version of the "time rule," a guideline that allocates the award based on what was earned during the marriage, typically by prorating the unvested awards based on when they were granted. But courts have often modified this rule so it applies only to awards issued for service performed during the marriage, as opposed to awards meant to be an inducement for future employment. Similar issues come up in alimony (and child support) disputes. Another problem is what valuation standard to use for options in the family law context (a standard that differs from that used in the contract damages context). One approach is to determine the value on exercise; another is to use a present value calculation at either grant or vesting.

This chapter is organized by state, as divorce litigation is entirely a matter of state law.

Arizona

Employer's intent a critical issue in dividing options

In *Brebaugh v. Deane*, 211 Ariz. 95 (Ariz. Ct. App.-Div. 1 2005), the Arizona Court of Appeals reversed the trial court on a finding that an employer's intent is critical in determining how to allocate unvested options in a community property state. The lower court, using the time rule applied in other cases regarding compensation, had held that unvested options were intended as incentives for future employment and thus were community property. Half the options were thus awarded to the non-employed spouse. The Court of Appeals agreed that the time rule was the appropriate standard but rejected its application at trial, reasoning that if options were intended as compensation for service with the employer during the time before the marriage's dissolution, then they were community property, but if they were intended as an inducement for future employment, they were not. That meant that the employer's intention in granting the option was critical. The court noted that only Texas and Wisconsin courts have held that unvested options are entirely community property.

Vested options count for child support

In *In re the Marriage of Robinson*, 201 Ariz. 328 (Ariz. Ct. App. 2002), an Arizona appeals court ruled that vested options earned during a marriage should be used in determining child support and that the trial court should have some discretion in how to value them. The husband claimed that options had no value until exercised, while his wife argued that allowing him to defer valuation until date of exercise gave him an unfair advantage in calculating his support payments. In fact, income from the exercise of options over a four-year period (from 1995 to 1998) represented many times his annual salary of $44,000 (totaling over $1 million in 1998 alone). The appellate court noted that there is no simple answer: valuation approaches could range from intrinsic value at the time of separation through a Black–Scholes value or constructive trust. The case was remanded for additional determinations by the trial court.

Arkansas

Income from future stock options includable in alimony settlement

In *Heitt v. Heitt*, No. 03-812 (Ark. Ct. App. Apr. 14, 2004), an Arkansas appeals court held that a former spouse's future stock options may be treated as income for purposes of alimony. At trial, the defendant argued that unvested stock options were necessarily excluded from divorce settlements by Arkansas law. The trial court, however, determined that the Heitt's divorce settlement had anticipated basing alimony on all future sources of income, specifically including vested and exercised options as reported on the employee's tax forms for a particular year.

California

Exercised stock options are includible in child support calculations

In *In re Nehk*, 2002 Cal. App. Unpub. LEXIS 1098 (May 14, 2002), the husband represented at the time of divorce that his stock options were part of his retirement plan and therefore excludable from income for purposes of determining child support. Five years later, the wife discovered that he had been exercising the options continuously and that income from such options did not constitute retirement income. She sued for an accounting and modification of child support obligations, but the trial court held her claims were time-barred. The appellate court reversed because of the husband's misrepresentation at time of divorce, holding that stock option gains should be treated as an includible bonus for these purposes.

Extra year added to time rule to account for vesting

In *Jones v. Steinberger* (*In re Marriage of Steinberger*), 91 Cal. App. 4th 1449 (Cal. Ct. App. 2001), *review denied* (2001), the court modified the California time rule to add an extra year. As a general rule, California courts determine community property interests by allocating a fraction of a spouse's options, the numerator of which is the length of service *during the marriage but before separation*, and the denominator of which is the total length of service by the employee-spouse. Community interest is then ascertained by multiplying this ratio times the total number of options. Here, the court included in the denominator a year that followed termination of employment and separation of the parties because the extra year counted toward option vesting in accordance with a severance agreement the employee-spouse reached with her employer after the parties separated.

Connecticut

Post-separation, pre-dissolution options are marital property

In *Kiniry v. Kiniry,* No. 21175 (Conn. App. Ct. Aug. 20, 2002), a Connecticut appellate court ruled that options received from a new employer by the former husband after separation but before dissolution are marital property. The wife filed for dissolution in February 1998; in October 1998, the husband lost his job. On January 3, 1999, he took a new job and was offered vested and unvested stock awards with Credit Suisse. The options were 25% vested immediately and 25% per year thereafter. The trial court awarded the spouse 60% of the options "if and when received." The husband appealed the decision. The appeals court ruled that the option documentation made it clear that both the vested and unvested options were a reward for current compensation in 1999 and thus divisible as marital property. The court distinguished this case from *Hopfer v. Hopfer* (discussed below) on the grounds that in that case the spouse was awarded unvested options that were for future service (in *Hopfer*, the court denied division of unvested options). The court also rejected the husband's argument that his former wife had not contributed to the earnings of the awards, saying that the wife had given up a lucrative job to raise the couple's children, thus making it possible for the spouse to pursue his career.

Unvested options not marital assets

In *Hopfer v. Hopfer*, 757 A.2d 673 (Conn. App. Ct. 2000), the court rejected a wife's arguments that husband's unvested options were marital property. The options had become effective just one month before the divorce settlement and were granted, in the court's view, purely as in incentive for his employment.

Florida

Stock options for future performance are not spouse's separate property

In *Ruberg v. Ruberg*, No. 2D01-2139 (Fla. Dist. Ct. App. Nov. 7, 2003), a Florida appellate court held that stock options and restricted shares granted for future performance are the property of the employed spouse. The employed spouse worked for Intermedia Communications (later acquired by WorldCom, Inc.), which had granted him options and restricted stock. The plan documents stated that the awards were meant to "attract, retain, and provide incentives to employees" and provide an incentive to further the interests of the employer. The options would stop vesting on termination. The trial court ruled that unvested options and restricted shares were for future performance and thus were not marital property. The judge distinguished this case from another Florida case, *Jensen v. Jensen*, 824 So. 2d 315 (Fla. Ct. App. 2002), in which a Cisco employee was granted options that, the court decided, were "for his past commendable service [but] contingent upon [his] continued service." There, the awards were a form of deferred compensation.

Maryland

Both vested and unvested options may be subject to division

In *Otley v. Otley*, 810 A.2d 1 (Ct. Spec. App. Md. 2002), the original dissolution judgment had excluded the husband's unexercised stock options from the marital estate. At the time of trial, 25% of the husband's options had vested, but the trial court held that because the options were unexercised they were not subject to valuation for purposes of division. On appeal, the appellate court reversed and remanded, holding that (1) both vested and unvested options are marital assets subject to division, (2) unvested options must be valued at the time of divorce, and (3) the time rule should be used to allocate options between former spouses.

Massachusetts

Unvested options are assets includible in marital estate

In *Baccanti v. Morton*, 434 Mass. 787 (2001), the Massachusetts Supreme Court held that unvested stock options were part of the marital estate even when granted for past services performed before the marriage. The court applied the time rule, as modified to reflect the fact that under Massachusetts law, property acquired before a marriage may be included in the marital estate. Accordingly, the rule was applied to the unvested options by multiplying the number of unvested options times a fraction whose numerator is the length of time the employee owned the options before dissolution of the marriage (i.e., the length of time the employee owned the options before *and during* the marriage), and whose denominator is the time between the date the options were issued and the date on which they were scheduled to vest. The product equals the amount of unvested options available for allocation between the parties.

Minnesota

Trial court has broad discretion to value options

In *In re Deviny*, 2002 Minn. App. LEXIS 1297 (Minn. Ct. App. 2002), the parties appealed the trial court's valuation of nontransferable options held by the husband as of the day before trial. The appellate court held that under Minnesota law, the trial judge has the ability to determine the most equitable valuation date.

Missouri

Stock options granted the day after divorce becomes final are not subject to division in divorce settlement

In *Clance v. Clance*, 127 S.W.3d 716 (Mo. Ct. App. 2004), a Missouri appeals court held that a trial court did not have jurisdiction to divide stock options a husband received the day after the divorce settlement became final. The divorce was granted on December 12, 2000. The next day, the husband received options on 2,500 shares of his employer. The trial court decided that the options were granted, in part, for prior performance and thus were marital property. The husband appealed, saying that the options did not exist until after the marriage was dissolved. The appellate court agreed, noting that notwithstanding the extreme result, there is no "safe harbor" for post-dissolution grants under Missouri law.

Options awarded before dissolution are marital property, even if unvested

In *Warner v. Warner*, 46 S.W.3d 591 (Mo. Ct. App. 2001), *motion for reh'g in transfer to Supreme Court denied* (2001), Charles and Sandra Warner dissolved their marriage on December 31, 1998. Charles Warner took a job at America Online (AOL) during the marriage dissolution proceedings and received options as part of his compensation. Sandra Warner then petitioned the court for a share of the options. A trial court divided the options between her and her husband. He appealed, but the appellate court concurred with the trial court. Charles Warner contended that his employment at AOL did not start until the trial in the proceedings had begun and, in any event that his options had not even started to vest. The court concluded that Missouri law made it clear that options obtained before dissolution were community property. The fact that they had not yet vested was outweighed by the fact that Charles Warner's previous work experience while married had made him a candidate to receive options. The decision did not indicate what formula was to be used to divide the options.

New Hampshire

Unvested options divided according to when they were earned

In *In re Valence*, No. 2000-395 (N.H. May 7, 2002), the New Hampshire Supreme Court ruled a "time-based" formula would be used to distribute options in a divorce. The husband had received stock options subject to vesting. When the divorce proceedings started, the husband had vested and unvested options. The trial court treated both kinds of options as divisible marital assets; the husband appealed, arguing that unvested options would vest only upon his continued employment. On appeal, the court noted that intangible property is considered marital property in New Hampshire. It held that unvested stock options represent intangible property and hence that they are divisible martial assets to the extent they were earned before dissolution of the marriage. The case was remanded with instructions for the trial court to allocate the options based on past and future services and then to divide the unvested options based on its determination of what percentage of these options were for service during the marriage. The wife's portion of the options, however, was to be delivered to her if and when they vest. The court made it clear it did not want to force the employee to exercise the options in order to meet the terms of the settlement.

New Jersey

Wife not entitled to half of options granted just before divorce

In *Robertson v. Robertson*, 381 N.J. Super. 199 (N.J. Super. App. Div. 2005), the New Jersey Superior Court, Appellate Division, held that the non-employee former spouse was not entitled to one-half of the options issued to her former husband as a signing and retention bonus three days before divorce papers were filed. The options vested over a four-year period. Mrs. Robertson argued that in a prior case, the New Jersey Supreme Court had held that while in dividing marital property, the date of filing for divorce should be a bright line to determine property division, cases should also be resolved on their own facts. Here, the wife maintained that her contributions to the marriage over the years should be recognized as a contribution to her husband's eligibility to receive more options. On review, the court held that the options were issued to Mr. Robertson as an inducement for future employment, not a reward for prior performance. Accordingly, the options were not compensation subject to equitable division for each party's contribution to the marriage.

Stock options granted after divorce excludable from child support calculation

In *Heller-Loren v. Appuzio,* No. A-0494-2T3 (N.J. App. Div. Aug. 3, 2004), a New Jersey appeals court reversed a trial court and held that a non-custodial parent did not have an obligation to include stock options awarded after the divorce in his calculation of income for child support purposes. Both former spouses received options during the marriage, and those options were expressly included in calculating their proportionate share of income at the time of settlement. Under New Jersey law, future earnings from options could certainly have been included in income for all purposes. However, the couple's property settlement agreement set out a specific list of items that would be included in "income" for purposes of computing future child support, and stock options were not on that list. Given the specificity of the contract, the custodial spouse could not now complain that the omission was inadvertent.

North Carolina
Court allows intrinsic value method for options in divorce case

In *Fountain v. Fountain,* No. 01-14 (N.C. Ct. App. Feb. 5, 2002), a North Carolina appellate court approved a lower court's decision to value stock options at their intrinsic value (the current fair market value minus the exercise price) rather than, as the wife had argued, using a Black-Scholes present value assessment. The court ruled that no standard for valuation of options had been adopted in the state, and that intrinsic value was acceptable in this light. The court also allowed the husband to pay for the value of the options due the wife in assets other than the right to exercise the option or receive value from the husband's future exercise of the options, arguing that taxes, transfer issues, and other concerns made it more practical to leave the options in the hands of the option holder and pay the spouse in other marital assets.

Ohio

Stock options granted during marriage are subject to division

In *Fox v. Fox*, 2002 Ohio 2010 (Ohio Ct. App. Apr. 25, 2002), the wife appealed from a judgment that did not include stock options in the marital estate. The parties had a prenuptial agreement that did not mention the options, which were granted pursuant to a stock option plan that existed before the marriage. The court held that stock option grants made during the marriage were new agreements between the husband and his employer, and so it remanded the case to determine whether the options were awarded for services provided during the marriage.

Pennsylvania

Parent's income includes unexercised vested options

In *Mackinley v. Messerchmidt*, No. 2137 EDA 2001 (Pa. Super. Ct. Nov. 18, 2002), a Pennsylvania Superior Court ruled that the unexercised vested options of a parent must count as available income for child support calculations, even if the parent chooses not to exercise them. The ruling reversed a trial court's conclusion that unexercised vested options do not count as income until the spouse exercises them, at which point they could be included for purposes of calculating child support. The trial court held that the other spouse could petition the court to force exercise if the spouse with the options failed to do so in a timely manner. The appellate court disagreed with the enforced exercise, noting that options can be subject to a present value analysis for these purposes. However, although the mother could not be forced to exercise, in Pennsylvania, the parent's obligations are based on "earnings capacity." Once the valuation was achieved, the mother would need to use other funds to satisfy her obligation. The court reasoned that if a parent chooses to earn an income lower than at the time of the marriage's dissolution, that parent must still maintain the support levels originally specified because she has the *capacity* to earn more; a child should not have to wait for a parent to realize income that is currently available.

Unvested options are marital assets

In *Fisher v. Fisher*, 564 Pa. 586 (Pa. 2001), the Pennsylvania Supreme Court ruled that stock options are marital assets. James and Patricia

Fisher were married in 1984, separated in 1993, and divorced in 1994. Fisher was an executive at Harley-Davidson and had $71,000 in unvested options. Patricia Fisher contended that she should receive a share of these unvested options when exercised. A trial court sided with the husband, but the Supreme Court reversed the ruling. The court concluded that unvested options were similar to unvested pension rights, rights that other states had included in divorce settlements. The court ruled, with dissenting opinions, that the value of the options should be divided if and when they are exercised. Dissenting opinions argued that the options should be valued at the time of divorce using some kind of present value approach and, in a separate opinion, that the wife should have some say in whether and when the options are exercised.

Washington

Stock option proceeds deposited in various investment accounts marital property

In *In re Marriage of Shui v. Rose*, No. 54539-6-I (Wash. Ct. App. Dec. 19, 2005), the Washington Court of Appeals ruled that proceeds from exercised options were still community property, even though some of the options themselves were community property and some separate property. The proceeds had been invested into various investment accounts, and it was impossible, the court found, to trace the origin of each dollar in the accounts back to the different group of options. By law, therefore, all the proceeds became community property.

The husband began receiving options from Microsoft in 1991 and was granted additional options in 1993 and 1994. He was married two months after the 1994 grant and continued to receive grants. In 1998 and 1999, he exercised options granted at various times, including options granted before marriage. He sold the shares for $6.5 million and invested the money in four investment accounts, only one of which was held jointly with his wife. In 2002, he was divorced. The trial court characterized 61% of the money as separate property. The wife appealed the ruling as to the pre-marriage options. The trial court said the time rule for options in Washington requires that for options granted before marriage, only those that vest after the marriage are community property. Because the assets had been invested in a way that mixed options subject to the time rule and those that were not, the husband simply assumed a percentage of the total option exercise proceeds equal to the value of the options that were separate in character under the time rule.

The appellate court, however, said that this was inadequate. Instead, the husband would have had to identify the invested assets that specifically came from the exercise of awards considered separate property. Because it was no longer possible to trace the remaining proceeds from option exercises to their respective separate or community sources with any particularity, the court ruled the entire amount was community property.

Options are community property, including increase in share value post-exercise

In *Chumbley v. Beckmann,* 110 Wash. App. 871, 43 P.3d 53 (Wash. Ct. App. 2002), *reversed and remanded,* No. 72539-0 (Wash. Aug. 14, 2003), a Washington appellate court ruled that options earned during a marriage, and any gains on them subsequently, were community property. Patricia Beckman worked for Immunex, which granted her options. She exercised some of the options with her own money from an inheritance. The trial court ruled that the proceeds from these options were hers alone. It awarded her husband Gerald Chumbley $51,000, his share of the increase in the value of the awards between grant and exercise, but it denied him any share of the subsequent stock appreciation.

The Court of Appeals reversed the ruling, concluding that the increase in the stock value was the result of market forces, not Beckmann's efforts. The purchase of the shares in question was accomplished with what was defined as community property, and thus the appreciation in those shares should be divided between the parties. On review, the Washington State Supreme Court reversed the appellate decision, holding that the use of separate property to acquire stock options in a community property state may result in gains on the stock being allocable to both community property and separate property. The court concluded, however, that the law in Washington already allows a spouse to manage assets alone, including community property (with some exceptions, of which options are not one), provided such management is in good faith for community interests. In this case, Beckmann said that the options would be lost if not exercised using the funds. The court concurred, concluding that the gains on the stock were, as the trial court found, both community and separate property, and it remanded the case to the trial court to make a pro rata distribution based on which part was separable and which part community.

Options valued as of date of vesting

In *Ayyad v. Rashid,* 2003 Wash. App. LEXIS 383 (Wash. Ct. App. Mar. 10, 2003), a Washington appellate court affirmed a lower court holding that unvested options may be valued for family law purposes as of the first date on which they could have been exercised. In the initial settlement agreement, the husband listed his vested options but not his unvested options. Four years later, the wife filed to vacate the agreement based on his failure to disclose the options, and ultimately the courts held in her favor. The issue finally before the trial court was how and when to value the options. After hearing testimony from the husband's expert, the court determined that the options could have been exercised when they first vested, and it awarded the wife half of the gain that would have represented, regardless of whether the husband actually did exercise when the options first vested. The court rejected the husband's argument that unvested options are "mere expectancies," saying that the expectancies in a marriage can be divided. (Note that in this case, the wife did not present competing expert testimony, so it is possible that another valuation argument could also have been persuasive.)

CHAPTER 6

Tax Litigation Arising from Equity Compensation Issues

Contents

1. **U.S. Tax Court Rulings** 62
   IRS need not compromise on AMT liability 62
   Exercise of option with third-party loan does not eliminate tax consequences under Section 83 63
   Blackout trading period not a substantial risk of forfeiture 64
   Tax on option exercise unaffected by Section 16 64
2. **State Tax Law Issues** 65
   California: Disposition of options by nonresident subject to California tax 65
   California: Taxes must be paid by nonresident on exercised options 66
   California: Stock transfer occurs notwithstanding margin loan 66
   New York: Gain on stock options must be allocated between New York and Washington 67
   New York: Nonresident's stock payments ruled to be New York source income 68

This chapter reviews recent federal and state tax cases related to equity compensation. To rise to the United States Tax Court, a taxpayer must have appealed the result of his or her tax audit up through all IRS administrative levels. Accordingly, the issues that arise for the federal courts frequently concern construction of difficult technical issues under the Internal Revenue Code (such as Section 83 and the alternative minimum tax). At the state level, the most common issue involves how income tax obligations must be divided between states when an employee works or has worked in one state and exercises the option in another. Generally, state courts will base their allocation on the same principles as those used to allocate foreign vs. domestic income sourcing at the federal level.

Please note that recent IRS administrative rulings and regulations are discussed in a separate chapter in Part II.

1. U.S. Tax Court Rulings

Several of the cases below represent attempts for taxpayers to get around the unfortunate results of the dot-com boom and bust. The rapidity with which stock prices fell during this period left many taxpayers with unanticipated tax bills and disputes that are still wending their way through the tax system.

IRS need not compromise on AMT liability

In *Speltz v. Commissioner,* 124 T.C. 9 (2005), the U.S. Tax Court upheld the IRS rejection of the taxpayer's compromise offer regarding the underpayment of alternative minimum tax (AMT) as a result of his stock option gains. Here, the taxpayer (Speltz) received incentive stock options (ISOs) as part of his compensation package. In 2000, his salary was just over $90,000, but the spread on exercise of his ISOs resulted in $711,118 of alternative minimum taxable income. Speltz ended up owing AMT of $206,191, but because the value of the stock dropped dramatically after exercise, he sold the shares for just under $77,000.

On audit, Speltz proposed a compromise settlement to the IRS, saying the couple's lifestyle was dramatically affected by the assessment: his wife needed to get a job, his oldest child had to switch schools, retirement savings were put off, charitable contributions were reduced, and the couple could not have a desired fourth child. Speltz argued that his tax amounted to 11 times what a similar taxpayer would pay on that amount of income if the actual sale price of the shares were used to determine income. Most importantly, he claimed that regulations under Section 7122 of the Internal Revenue Code (the "Code") trump the literal application of the rules for collection of taxes. Those regulations state that a compromise can be entered into where collection in full could be achieved but would constitute unreasonable economic hardship and impede effective tax administration.

Unfortunately for Speltz, the Tax Court deferred to the IRS for guidelines on what constitutes an unacceptable reduction in the standard of living, guidelines that could be well below a family's current standard. The court noted that the literal application of the AMT does create hardships in many cases, but courts have consistently rejected claims that this was inequitable. Congress, the court noted, is well aware of the problem but has not chosen to do anything about it so far.

Exercise of option with third-party loan does not eliminate tax consequences under Section 83

In *Hilen v. Commissioner*, T.C.M. 2005-226 (2005), the U.S. Tax Court held that a taxpayer must pay taxes on the exercise of nonstatutory options (NSOs) even though he had financed their exercise with personal nonrecourse loans from a bank. Keith Hilen received options during a four-year period with his employer. In 1999, he exercised his options, borrowing money from a bank to pay for the exercise. His shares were pledged as collateral. The company went public that year, and Hilen could not sell the shares until January 2000, although he received voting rights and dividends during the several-month period between his exercise and the end of the restriction. In 1999, he recorded the spread on the options as income. The company's shares performed poorly, and Hilen soon thereafter filed for bankruptcy, defaulting on the bank loan. He then filed an amended return, claiming that because he never made a payment on the loan, he did not bear the risk of the shares' decline. His attorneys relied on Treas. Reg. § 1.83-3(a) (7), which states that "the grant of an option to purchase certain property does not constitute the receipt of such property." The taxpayer argued (creatively!) that under the regulation, if any debt is incurred for the purchase, it results in the grant being deemed ineffective.

The court disagreed, noting first that the issue here was not the *grant* of the option but its *exercise*. Second, third-party debt is not equivalent to debt to the company. How the taxpayer financed the shares is irrelevant. Moreover, he had actually received shares, not options, upon exercise and had voting and dividend rights on those shares. The court also rejected the notion that the proper date of transfer was when the IPO-related restrictions lapsed (as have many courts before this). Finally, the court cited Treas. Reg. § 1.83-(c)(1) for the proposition that the risk that the value of the shares will decline (notwithstanding restrictions on sale) does not constitute a substantial risk of forfeiture for purposes of Code Section 83.

Blackout trading period not a substantial risk of forfeiture

In *Merlo v. Commissioner*, T.C.M. 2005-178 (2005), the U.S. Tax Court ruled against petitioner Merlo on summary judgment, holding that there was no issue of material fact as to whether the petitioner's rights to shares were subject to a substantial risk of forfeiture when the only limitation on his sale of previously acquired ISO stock was the issuer's blackout period. Merlo had exercised his ISO at the end of 2000 (at the time of his termination), but he failed to take into account the AMT preference on his tax return. On audit, he claimed that the preference was inapplicable because the shares were subject to a substantial risk of forfeiture under Section 83 in the form of the blackout period. Because ISOs are treated as NSOs for purposes of the AMT, Merlo argued that no AMT preference could arise until the blackout period was lifted. He relied on *Robinson v. Commissioner* (which held that a substantial risk of forfeiture arises when the company has a one-year call on the shares after termination) in making his argument. The Tax Court noted that Merlo was not a Section 16 insider (which could raise Section 83(c) arguments in favor of forfeiture), nor did the issuer have the ability to compel him to return his shares if he traded during the blackout period. Without more, there was no indication that he had a "substantial risk of losing the rights to his shares." Summary judgment was granted in favor of the government. For a similar development, see the discussion of Rev. Rul. 2005-48 below.

Tax on option exercise unaffected by Section 16

In *Tanner v. Commissioner*, 2003 U.S. App. LEXIS 7926 (5th Cir. Mar. 26, 2003), the U.S. Court of Appeals for the Fifth Circuit affirmed the U.S. Tax Court's holding that an optionee was required to include in ordinary income the amount realized on exercise of a nonstatutory stock option for vested stock regardless of whether the stock was subject to certain contractual restrictions on sale. In general, Section 83 of the Code requires an optionee to include income at the time that property is transferred to him or her free of a "substantial risk of forfeiture." Section 83(c)(3) of the Code provides that stock will be deemed subject to a substantial risk of forfeiture during the period in which the holder is subject to the "short-swing profit" restrictions of Section 16(b) of the Securities Exchange Act.

In this case, Tanner was CEO and president of a public company and had substantial nonqualified options in the company. His option agreements provided that upon exercise, all shares would be subject to a two-year lock-up agreement in addition to any Section 16(b) restrictions imposed by the Act. Tanner exercised his options but did not include income at the time of exercise, arguing that the contractual provisions effectively extended the Section 16 short-swing profit period from six months to two years, thus providing a two-year period within which his stock was subject to a substantial risk of forfeiture under Section 83(c)(3). Under this reasoning, income would not be includable until two years after exercise.

The Tax Court disagreed, finding that Section 16(b) was irrelevant to the tax analysis because for securities law purposes, Section 16 restrictions begin on the date of grant and expire six months later. Because the option was granted more than six months before the exercise, the Section 16(b) restrictions had no Section 83 implications for this case. Moreover, the court specifically held that for purposes of Section 83(c)(3), the six-month period provided by Section 16(b) cannot be extended by contract.

2. State Tax Law Issues

As one might expect, two states with high income taxes and active business communities—California and New York—face the most appeals from taxpayers on equity-related issues.

California: Disposition of options by nonresident subject to California tax

In *In re Cower* (No. 294394, Sept. 20, 2005), the California State Board of Equalization held that a nonresident who received compensation for services in California had to pay taxes on that compensation, including any compensation from the exercise of nonqualified options. The taxpayers argued that they exercised the options after they left the state, so it was not California source income. The CSBE concluded that the issue is whether the options were awarded for service provided in the state, not where the taxpayer exercised them.

California: Taxes must be paid by nonresident on exercised options

In *In re Randall* (No. 260104, Mar. 22, 2005), the California State Board of Equalization held that a nonresident individual must pay taxes on the exercise of stock options earned while he was a resident of California. The taxpayer earned ISOs while serving as the CEO of a California company, but he had moved out of state by the time of exercise. The CSBE noted that income earned in the state is taxable because under California law, income earned "is sourced to the state or states where the compensation was earned."

California: Stock transfer occurs notwithstanding margin loan

In *Miller v. United States*, No. C 04-0511 JSW (N.D. Cal. Nov. 22, 2004), the U.S. District Court for the Northern District of California ruled against the taxpayer on a motion for summary judgment on his tax refund claim. Miller was a Microsoft employee who in 2000 did a cashless exercise for vested options with a margin loan from PaineWebber and paid taxes on the spread at exercise. By 2003, the stock price had fallen sufficiently to result in a margin call, and PaineWebber sold the shares. Proving that hope and bad legal advice spring eternal, Miller filed for a tax refund, essentially arguing that the margin feature prevented the original transaction from closing for purposes of Section 83 of the Code. Under this novel argument (which the court duly noted as "a case of first impression"), Miller claimed that his exercise was actually deferred until the date sale—i.e., the stock was transferred to PaineWebber but not to him on the original exercise. Because the stock had lost its original value at the time of the margin call, Miller contended that there was no gain on exercise and accordingly his original tax payment should be refunded in full.

The court reviewed the established law and regulations with respect to Section 83 transfers (including transferability and substantial risk of forfeiture principles), and concluded that beneficial ownership in the shares was clearly transferred to Miller at the time of his exercise in 2000. Among other things, the court noted that the shares carried voting and dividend rights and that Miller had been able to make other investments based on the collateral in the margin account. Moreover, the regulations clearly indicate that the ability to pledge shares (e.g., for a margin loan) does not undermine beneficial ownership. Finally, the court noted that regardless of who actually wrote the check for the shares (i.e., Miller or PW) at the time of exercise, Microsoft received the exercise price and transferred the shares on Miller's account.

New York: Gain on stock options must be allocated between New York and Washington

In *In the Matter of the Petition of E. Randall Stuckless and Jennifer Olson,* DTA 819319 (N.Y. Div. of Tax App. July 8, 2004), the New York State Division of Tax Appeals upheld a state tax determination that a portion of the income received by a taxpayer from the exercise of stock options granted during his New York employment was subject to tax as New York source income, even though the exercise occurred while the taxpayer was a nonresident. Taxpayer Stuckless had appealed a New York state tax assessment on income earned from options granted to him while he was a New York resident but exercised while he was resident in Washington State. Stuckless was a New York Microsoft employee who was granted ISOs in 1991 and 1992. He transferred to Washington State in 1996 and exercised most of his previously granted (and fully vested) options between 1996 and 1998 while resident in Washington. He moved back to New York in mid-1998.

Stuckless tried a number of arguments on appeal (including that, notwithstanding federal tax precedent, the options were investment vehicles rather than compensatory options). His most important argument was that option income should be sourced to the state where the exercise occurred regardless of whether services were rendered elsewhere. However, the court looked to Sections 83 and 422 of the Code for the principle that income received on the exercise of vested options represents compensation for services rendered. In Stuckless's case, the court agreed with the New York Division of Taxation that Stuckless owed New York state taxes on the percentage of income allocable to his performance of services for Microsoft while a New York resident: i.e., the number of days worked while resident in New York over the total number of days worked. (Note: this is the same formula the IRS uses when allocating option gain between U.S. and foreign source income.)

New York: Nonresident's stock payments ruled to be New York source income

In *In re Clapes,* N. 818992 (N.Y. Div. of Tax Appeals Sept. 18, 2003), the New York Division of Tax Appeals held that income from a former IBM employee's stock options were New York source income. In 1995, Clapes was passed over at IBM for a younger employee for the position of general counsel. He resigned in 1996 under an early retirement plan. IBM agreed to pay him his remaining salary, cash for long-term performance stock, stock options, and a cash bonus. Clapes did not report these payments as income for the next three years. The New York Division of Tax assessed him for taxes due. Clapes petitioned for a rehearing, arguing that the payments were not for past or current work but instead were compensation for the loss of future income resulting from age discrimination. The Division of Tax Appeals concluded that the income did derive from his work in New York for IBM. The age discrimination issue was not relevant because Clapes signed a release from IBM relinquishing the right to make claims about the issue, among other things, and the releases were expressly included in the early retirement plan's summary plan description. Clapes also had not made any age discrimination claims against IBM.

Part II:
Recent Administrative Rulings and Regulations

CHAPTER 7

IRS Rulings on Equity Compensation

Contents

1. **Corporate Matters** 72
   Rev. Rul. 2003-98: Deductibility of options after grantor company is acquired 73
   Notice 2005-99: Restricted stock and restricted stock units can be accounted for under cost-sharing arrangements 73
   Rec. Rul. 2001-1: Corporate deductions for exercise of nonqualified options not subject to AMT 74
   PLR 200550007: Cashless exercise program does not affect Section 162(m) calculation 74

2. **Individual Matters** 75
   Rev. Rul. 2005-48: Income from options must be recognized despite stock sale restrictions 75
   Rev. Rul. 2004-60, Rev. Rul. 2002-22, and Notice 2002-31: Transfers of nonstatutory stock options and nonqualified deferred compensation pursuant to divorce 76
   Rev. Rul. 2004-37: IRS issues ruling on reducing debt under promissory notes used for option exercise 78
   PLR 200032017: Vested nonqualified stock options are not parachute payments 79

3. **Stock Plan Administration** 79
   Rev. Rul. 2004-60: Transfer of options in divorce 79
   PLR 200551015: Amendment to ISO plan does not require shareholder approval 79
   PLR 200513012: Incentive stock option plan with ESPP-like features qualifies 80

71

72 | The Law of Equity Compensation

> Rev. Proc. 2002-50: IRS exempts brokers from certain stock option reporting requirements..80
>
> PLR 200207005: IRS allows paperless exercise of options 81

4. **Section 423 ESPPs** 81

> PLR 200547007: Amendment to ESPP excluding non–W-2 employees does not affect plan qualification..81
>
> PLR 200418020: Reduction in offering period not a "modification"..........82
>
> PLR 200241001: Date of grant in an ESPP is start of offering period even if employee buys shares with a lump-sum payment........................82
>
> PLR 200244006: ESPP can offer special purchase and entry dates to accommodate merger without shareholder approval 83
>
> PLR 200102042: Plan that has a first refusal right qualifies under Section 423 83

5. **Tax Shelters** 84

> Announcement 2005-19: Settlement initiative for stock option tax shelter scheme 84
>
> Rev. Rul. 2004-37: IRS shuts down purchase price adjustment scheme . 85

The Internal Revenue Service (IRS) issues a variety of rulings on tax matters in response to legislative mandates, technical audit requests by agents, and requests by individual taxpayers. There is a formal hierarchy to the rulings. Regulations interpret the Internal Revenue Code and are mandated by Congress: these have the force of law. Revenue rulings are citable and represent the official government position on issues, and, while given deference by the courts, do not have the same definitive weight as regulations. Private rulings, including private letter rulings (PLRs), technical advice memoranda (TAMs), and General Counsel memoranda, analyze and apply only to the facts at hand. Such private rulings have no precedential value, but practitioners use them as an indication of how the IRS would rule on similar issues in the future.

1. Corporate Matters

This section includes rulings that relate to corporate deductions and allocations.

Rev. Rul. 2003-98: Deductibility of options after grantor company is acquired

In Rev. Rul. 2003-98, 2003-34 I.R.B.378 (Aug. 25, 2003), the IRS reviewed four post-acquisition scenarios for the purpose of determining how to allocate compensation deductions related to compensatory stock options under Section 83 of the Code. Under Section 83(h), the service recipient (generally, the employer/grantor) may take a deduction in the year that the service provider includes an amount in ordinary income related to the option. When an acquiring company (the "acquiror") acquires the grantor company (the "target") and ordinary income related to stock options arises after the acquisition (whether through sale, cancellation, or exercise of the options), which company is entitled to the deduction? The IRS concluded that the allocation of the deduction depends on the form of the acquisition. If the target survives the acquisition (e.g., as a wholly owned subsidiary), then only the target may take the deduction. However, if the acquisition is in the form of a merger in which the target is liquidated and the acquiror survives, then the acquiror is entitled to the deduction.

Notice 2005-99: Restricted stock and restricted stock units can be accounted for under cost-sharing arrangements

In Notice 2005-99 (Dec. 27, 2005), the IRS announced that for purposes of allocations with respect to qualified cost-sharing arrangements (QCSAs), companies may use the same elective method for timing and measurement of restricted stock and restricted stock units (RSUs) as is now available for stock options. QCSAs are arrangements that permit U.S. multinational companies to allocate intangible costs among members of a controlled group of companies in different countries. Regulations issued in 2003 for stock options (Treas. Reg. § 1.482-7(d)(2)(iii)(B)) require that all costs for intangible development be taken into account. Generally, companies account for the costs at the time they are incurred. Before Notice 2005-99, companies could elect to measure the cost of stock options (but not other forms of equity compensation) based on GAAP principles for determining fair market value at grant. To qualify for this election, the underlying shares must be publicly traded and not subject to market conditions or significant post-vesting restrictions under FASB Statement of Financial Accounting Standards No. 123(R).

The 2003 regulations were issued to clarify how U.S. multinational companies allocate costs in cost-sharing arrangements with members of control groups. There was concern at the time about how these allocations were being made and whether costs were being shifted to maximize tax benefits for the U.S. parent. Normally, under GAAP rules, costs are recorded so that they were allocated to the same area (such as research and development) at the same time as the employee-recognized income. The IRS noted that with options that vest over time, these activities and costs are not necessarily the same as those simply recorded for the period as research and development, nor are they all necessarily attributable to work on the intangibles in question. For instance, an employee may receive a vested award in 2005 that was granted in 2001, during which time there was work on the intangibles in question as well as on other projects. That created considerable complexity in allocating costs.

To address this issue for stock option allocation, the 2003 regulations permit issuers to record the cost on the grant date, consistent with fair value accounting procedures, so long as the allocation analysis includes the activities and compensation of an employee during a reporting period. Thus, if an employee receives an option grant during a time in which he or she was working on a development project, the cost might be recorded at the time of grant based on its GAAP fair market value. A four-prong test (set out in the regulations) must be met to satisfy the requirement for the election. Notice 2005-99 extends this election for stock options to restricted stock and RSUs granted after December 8, 2005.

Rec. Rul. 2001-1: Corporate deductions for exercise of nonqualified options not subject to AMT

In Rev. Rul. 2001-1 (Feb. 26, 2001), the IRS ruled that the deductions a corporation takes on the spread of an exercise of nonqualified stock options are not disallowed as a deduction for purposes of computing the alternative minimum tax (AMT).

PLR 200550007: Cashless exercise program does not affect Section 162(m) calculation

In PLR 200550007 (Aug. 29, 2005), the IRS ruled that the amendment of a stock option plan to permit optionees to elect to use a net (cashless) exercise method does not adversely modify options that otherwise qualify as performance-based compensation for purposes of the "million-dollar cap" under Section 162(m) of the Code. The taxpayer also requested a ruling on whether the amendment would implicate Section 409A; the IRS indicated (correctly) that this is a "no-ruling" area and declined to comment.

2. Individual Matters

This section reviews rulings with respect to option exercises and related stock sales by individual taxpayers.

Rev. Rul. 2005-48: Income from options must be recognized despite stock sale restrictions

In Revenue Ruling 2005-48 (Aug. 5, 2005), the IRS ruled that an employee could not delay taxation on the exercise of nonstatutory stock options even though the options were subject to (1) a six-month lockup period before the employee could sell the shares under company rules limiting insider trading and (2) a risk of lawsuit (before exercise) under Section 16 of the Securities Exchange Act of 1934 (the "1934 Act") for any potential violation of securities laws. The employee was granted options in January 2005. In May 2005, the company went public. Pursuant to an underwriting agreement, the employee could not sell the shares until the end of November. An insider trading compliance policy established by the company allowed insiders, such as this employee, to trade company shares only between November 5 and November 30.

In August, the employee exercised the options and paid cash for the shares. In addition to the lockup period rules, as an insider the employee was subject to insider trading rules under Section 10b-5 of the 1934 Act. The employee contended that taxes should not be due on the option exercise because of the various restrictions on selling the shares. Under Code Section 83(c)(3), taxes are not due on the receipt of an award such as an option as long as the award is subject to a substantial risk of forfeiture, including the risk of a taxpayer lawsuit under Section 16(b) of the 1934 Act for violation of insider trading rules.

In *Robinson v. Commissioner,* 44 T.C. 20 (1965), the First Circuit Court of Appeals concluded that such risks as apply in this case were sufficient to delay taxation until they lapse. The IRS, however, rejected that reasoning here and (in information with the release of the ruling) said it would rely on it only for cases in the First Circuit. In requiring taxation, the IRS argued that the period of risk for a lawsuit under Section 16 applies to the six-month period from the *grant* of the option, not the exercise. That period could be even shorter if there is some other available exemption from the rules during the six-month period. Because the employee exercised in August, eight months after grant, the IRS concluded that there was no substantial remaining risk. The risks of any further securities lawsuits and/or the decline in value, the IRS concluded, were not sufficient to cause a significant risk of forfeiture under Section 83. Moreover, the restrictions imposed for compliance with insider trading rules and the lockup provisions were "non-lapse" restrictions that did not affect the taxability of the award under Section 83.

Rev. Rul. 2004-60, Rev. Rul. 2002-22, and Notice 2002-31: Transfers of nonstatutory stock options and nonqualified deferred compensation pursuant to divorce

The rules regarding tax treatment of option and nonqualified deferred compensation (NQDC) interests incident to divorce has undergone considerable revision in the last few years. These three rulings (when read together with the final ISO regulations) address timing, withholding, and reporting issues for income tax, FICA, and FUTA.

In Rev. Rul. 2002-22, 2002-1 C.B. 849, the IRS issued its first set of new rules for the taxation of NSOs in a divorce settlement. (The ruling applied to NSOs only because ISOs cannot be transferred in a separate property state; that is, an ISO becomes an NSO upon such a transfer.) The ruling changed a position the IRS had taken in a Field Service Advisory (FSA No. 2000005006), in which it had concluded that when an employee transfers an option to a spouse in a divorce settlement, the *employee* recognizes income. It was not clear whether the FSA applied only to community property states. In Rev. Rul. 2002-22, the IRS reversed the position taken in the FSA and ruled that there was no income to the employee at the time the option was transferred to or exercised by the non-employee former spouse (NEFS). Further, Rev. Rul. 2002-22 ruled that the transfer of options would not be a taxable event to either spouse, whether in a community property state or not. Instead, at the time the NEFS exercises the option, he or she would recognize income just as the employee would have had the employee exercised the option. Rev. Rul. 2002-22 applied prospectively, effective November 8, 2002.

On the same date, the IRS issued a proposed revenue ruling in Notice 2002-31 to impose income tax and payroll (FICA, Medicare, and FUTA) tax withholding on the NEFS at time of exercise, rather than on the employee spouse. The proposed ruling provided that the company issue a Form 1099 to the NEFS, withholding a sufficient amount of stock from his or her exercise to pay the relevant taxes. The company would then include the amount of the spread on the NEFS's exercise in the employee's FICA wages on Form W-2, giving credit to the employee for the spouse's FICA payment. Accordingly, if the employee's income exceeded the FICA wage base, neither the NEFS nor the employee would be subject to FICA (although both would be subject to Medicare tax).

In Rev. Rul. 2004-60 (June 14, 2004), the IRS provided final, comprehensive guidance on withholding, reporting, and tax issues relating to transfers incident to a divorce, effective January 1, 2005. The ruling concludes, as did the 2002 rulings, that NSOs and NQDC transferred by an employee to an NEFS incident to a divorce are subject to FICA, FUTA, and income tax withholding on the NEFS to the same extent as if retained by the employee. The fact setting considered is the same as that set out in Rev. Rul. 2002-22. There, the taxpayer employee transferred one-third of the total option grant to the NEFS. The IRS ruled on the following points:

1. For FICA (Social Security and Medicare) and FUTA (unemployment) tax purposes, the transfer of the options in and of itself is not considered the payment of income to the NEFS. At the date of exercise by the NEFS, however, the spread is subject to FICA just as it would be if exercised by the employee spouse. This means that if the employee spouse has already exceeded the FICA withholding ceiling, then the exercise by the NEFS will not result in additional FICA withholding. The employee portion of FICA is actually deducted from the payments to the NEFS, not from payments to the employee spouse. Because the employer pays all of the FUTA tax, the NEFS obviously has no responsibility for FUTA.

2. For federal income tax purposes, when the NEFS exercises the options, the employer must withhold taxes. The supplemental wage flat rate (25% of amounts of $1 million or less, and 35% of amounts in excess of $1 million) may be used for this withholding. The NEFS is entitled to use this amount as a credit when computing income taxes.

3. For reporting purposes, any FICA tax withholding is reported on form W-2 using the employee spouse's name, address, and Social Security number. However, no income is included in Box 1 or Box 2 with respect to these taxes. Instead, income received by the NEFS is reported in Box 3 on a Form 1099-MISC as "other income," and income tax withheld is reported in Box 4. The employer files a Form 945 to record income tax withholding for the NEFS, while FICA is reported on the employer's Form 941 and FUTA on Form 940.

Rev. Rul. 2004-60 expands on the conclusion of Rev. Rul. 2002-22 that a taxpayer who transfers interests in an NSO or NQDC to a NEFS incident to divorce is not required to include an amount in gross income on the transfer or exercise. Rev. Rul. 2004-60 also revises and adopts the proposed revenue ruling originally set out in Notice 2002-31 regarding withholding and reporting, effective as of January 1, 2005. For court orders or agreements entered before 2005, taxpayers may show good-faith reliance on Notice 2002-31 for reporting purposes.

Rev. Rul. 2004-37: IRS issues ruling on reducing debt under promissory notes used for option exercise

In Rev. Rul. 2004-37 (Feb. 26, 2004), the IRS ruled that an employee who issues a recourse note to his or her employer in satisfaction of the exercise price of an option to acquire employer stock will recognize compensation income under Section 83 of the Code if and when the parties subsequently agree to reduce the stated principal amount of the note. The facts in the ruling describe a typical "post-bubble" scenario: the taxpayer/employee used a full-recourse promissory note to exercise options for employer stock that later plunged underwater. When the note came due, the employer agreed to reduce the principal amount due to the stock's current value. The IRS rejected the taxpayer's argument that this type of reduction should be treated as a (nontaxable) purchase price reduction rather than a significant modification to the note resulting in (taxable) debt forgiveness. Rev. Rul. 2004-37 effectively shuts down this reporting position, which has become popular with corporate executives in recent years.

PLR 200032017: Vested nonqualified stock options are not parachute payments

The IRS ruled in PLR 200032017 (Aug. 11, 2000) that vested options in a company that is being acquired do not constitute parachute payments for the employees receiving them. The options were subject to a complex exchange formula that gave holders a higher-than-market price on conversion, but lower than what they would have been worth if the merger did not occur. Unvested options that vest on completion of the merger would also not be treated as parachute payments because they had a one-year vesting provision, enough to convince the court that the acceleration of vesting on completion of the merger was not additional compensation.

3. Stock Plan Administration

In recent years the IRS has issued a number of helpful rulings discussing the mechanics of plan administration.

Rev. Rul. 2004-60: Transfer of options in divorce

See discussion in Section 2 above.

PLR 200551015: Amendment to ISO plan does not require shareholder approval

In PLR 200551015 (Sept. 14, 2005), the IRS ruled that a board amendment to a plan that extended the time period within which ISOs could be granted under the plan did not require shareholder approval under Section 422(b). The plan had received shareholder approval previously for a different amendment, but at the time of the approval, the authorization to grant ISOs would have expired before the date later set by the board of directors. The IRS noted that shareholder approval results in a deemed re-adoption of a plan, with a statutory term of 10 years from the date of such approval. Because shareholder approval is required only to increase the number of shares available under the plan or to change the class of employees eligible to receive options, the board was free to adopt any other amendment consistent with the statutory requirements without a new approval.

PLR 200513012: Incentive stock option plan with ESPP-like features qualifies

In PLR 200513012 (April 1, 2005), the IRS ruled that a company's ISO plan qualified under Code Section 422. The plan was structured more like a Section 423 ESPP than a traditional option plan. Employees could enroll in the plan during a one-month enrollment period, during which time they could decide how much of their after-tax payroll they wanted to set aside on a regular basis to acquire shares later. The first day of the enrollment period was the grant date, which set the exercise price. The purchase price was the price at the end of the offering period, and the options had a one-year term. Employees could exercise at the end of one year, but they then had to transfer the shares to a bank-operated nominee account for at least one more year (which would allow them to meet ISO holding period requirements).

Rev. Proc. 2002-50: IRS exempts brokers from certain stock option reporting requirements

In Rev. Proc. 2002-50, the IRS provided an exemption from the 1099-B reporting requirements for stockbrokers handling the sale of shares acquired through options by employees, former employees, or other people providing a service to a company who engage in same-day sale transactions. Form 1099-B covers proceeds from broker and barter exchange transactions. To meet the exemption rules:

- The transaction must be executed the same day the stock is acquired through the option;
- The options must be covered by Section 83(b) of the Code and be granted in conjunction with services performed for a company;

- The optionee must certify in writing to the broker that the optionee will report to the employing company any compensation resulting from the exercise and/or disposition of the option;
- There must either be no commission or fee for the transaction, or, if there is, the broker must provide a written statement to the optionee detailing the charges; and
- The optionee must use the sale price for the shares to calculate the compensation element for reporting to the company; brokers can rely on a written statement from the optionee to verify this.

If a fee is involved, the broker must provide the gross sales price for shares sold through the broker, commissions and fees, and a description of how the optionee should report gains or losses with respect to exercised options on federal income tax filings.

PLR 200207005: IRS allows paperless exercise of options

In PLR 200207005 (Feb. 15, 2002), the IRS considered a case in which a company allowed its employees to exercise their stock options (ISOs and NSOs) via email sent over its corporate network. Employees can designate shares owned to be used by providing certificate numbers or by attesting to the number of shares to be sold if a broker holds the shares in "street name." The IRS ruled that this procedure is a constructive delivery of payment for the option exercise and does not constitute a modification of the plan's terms requiring shareholder approval

4. Section 423 ESPPs

PLR 200547007: Amendment to ESPP excluding non-W-2 employees does not affect plan qualification

In PLR 200547007 (Aug. 12, 2005), the IRS ruled that a shareholder-approved amendment to exclude independent contractors or employees of other companies who do not receive a W-2 from the sponsoring company's employee stock purchase plan (ESPP) does not negatively affect the plan's qualified status. In the event that any such employee is subsequently determined to be a common-law employee of the company, the ordinary eligibility thresholds under Section 423 (i.e., employees must work for the company for two years, work more than 20 hours per week, customarily work seven months per year or more, and not be "highly compensated employees" as defined in Section 414(q)) apply as of the date of such determination only.

PLR 200418020: Reduction in offering period not a "modification"

In PLR 200418020 (Apr. 30, 2004), the IRS ruled on a shareholder approval issue for an ESPP plan in which the taxpayer company amended its plan because it failed to file a timely Form S-8 registration. The taxpayer company offered a conventional ESPP with a 15% discount, a six-month offering period, and a look-back feature. It was required to register its ESPP stock on a Form S-8, but it missed the applicable deadline. Because the options issued under the plan must be covered by a registration statement, the company had to suspend the plan until the new statement was filed. The company thus amended its plan to extend its current offering period for an additional quarter while suspending the current purchase period until the registration was effective. The plan also was amended to require employees to notify the company of any disqualifying dispositions of stock acquired through the plan, and to provide that the gain would be subject to withholding.

Under ESPP rules, a "material modification" to a Section 423 ESPP must be approved by shareholders. Because the modification at issue simply exchanged the right to exercise in the current quarter for a right to exercise in a later quarter, the IRS ruled that the amendment did not increase benefits and therefore was not a material modification for shareholder approval purposes. The changes related to disqualifying dispositions were simply minor technical changes and also did not rise to the level of material modification.

PLR 200241001: Date of grant in an ESPP is start of offering period even if employee buys shares with a lump-sum payment

In PLR 200241001 (Oct. 11, 2002), the IRS ruled on an ESPP in which the company established four-consecutive three-month purchase periods.

The plan met Section 423 rules. It defined base pay as monthly wages and salary, plus average monthly tips, but not overtime or bonuses. Contributions to 401(k) plans or Section 125 plans did not reduce base pay. The IRS ruled that this definition of base pay was acceptable. The plan also provided that employees could purchase shares during the purchase period by making a one-time lump-sum payment. The IRS ruled that this was acceptable.

PLR 200244006: ESPP can offer special purchase and entry dates to accommodate merger without shareholder approval

In PLR 200244006 (Nov. 11, 2002), the IRS ruled on an ESPP involved in a merger. The company being acquired and the acquirer both had ESPPs. The companies agreed that the purchase date for the ESPP of the acquired company would be moved up to the completion date of the merger or, if more practical, the last payroll date immediately before that. Employees could then exercise their options to purchase shares. The shares would be converted into shares of the acquiring company. Employees of the acquired company who become employees of the acquirer would be able to participate in the acquirer's ESPP on the next May 1 entry date after the merger or, if the merger occurred after May 1, a special entry date just for these employees. The IRS approved this arrangement, saying that the special entry and purchase date features did not constitute a new plan that would have to be approved by shareholders.

PLR 200102042: Plan that has a first refusal right qualifies under Section 423

A company's Section 423 ESPP allows employees to purchase shares at a 15% discount at either the end or the beginning of its offering period. Once employees have purchased the shares, they must provide the employer notification of their intent to sell the stock if the sale is to occur within two years after the grant of the right to purchase or one year after exercise. The company then has 10 days to repurchase the shares at the lower of the price at which they bought them or the current market price. If the repurchase occurs, the deduction to the employer and the taxable amount to the employee are determined by the actual price paid for the shares. In PLR 200102042 (Jan. 12, 2001), the IRS ruled that this plan would qualify under Section 423 of the Code.

5. Tax Shelters

The huge run-up in the stock market in the dot-com boom prompted an unusual number of creative, if not especially responsible, tax shelter arrangements. The rulings below deal with some of the major ones, but the IRS has now adopted a much more aggressive stance on these kinds of practices that have no valid purpose other than tax reduction.

Announcement 2005-19: Settlement initiative for stock option tax shelter scheme

In Announcement 2005-19 (Mar. 15, 2005), as modified by Announcement 2005-39 (Mar. 22, 2005), the IRS issued settlement guidance on a stock option tax avoidance scheme that was popular with executives during prior years. Taxpayers who had used the scheme were given until May 23, 2005, to agree to the settlement; otherwise, the IRS would pursue a claim. Taxpayers who resolved their tax issues under Announcement 2005-19 do not have to disclose these deals under Section 6011 of the Code for taxable years ending in 2004 or any subsequent years.

The tax avoidance scheme at issue (which was ultimately addressed in 2004 regulations under Section 83) worked like this: (1) the optionee sold an unexercised nonqualified option to a relative or family limited partnership in which he had a substantial interest in exchange for a long-term unsecured note; (2) the new holder exercised the option later (recognizing gain only on a subsequent sale); and (3) the optionee deferred tax until balloon payments were finally made under the note (as much as 15 to 30 years later). In effect, the optionee received the tax deferral benefit of an ISO, minus the AMT obligation, while actually retaining control over the option through the relationship with the related party. Under Section 83 and its regulations, a transfer of property will not "close" the tax transaction unless the transfer is the equivalent of an arm's-length sale; these clearly were not. On October 15, 2004, the IRS posted an issue paper on its Web site that described its views on the scheme in more detail, arguing it was a sham transaction intended simply to avoid taxes.

Rev. Rul. 2004-37: IRS shuts down purchase price adjustment scheme

In Revenue Ruling 2004-37 (Feb. 25, 2004), the IRS shut down an aggressive strategy whereby taxpayers took the position that certain forms of compensation-related loan forgiveness could result in nontaxable purchase price adjustments. The strategy revolved around the following scenario: (1) the taxpayer receives a loan from his or her employer to exercise an option; (2) the loan requires only interest payments to be made, with principal due at the end of the term; (3) when the stock value drops while the loan is outstanding, the principal is reduced ("adjusted") to reflect the new value; (4) loan forgiveness is *not* recorded for the adjustment.

The ruling summarized the fact pattern as follows:

> In Year 1, Employer, a corporation, grants a nontransferable, nonstatutory option to its Employee to purchase 1,000 shares of Employer common stock at an exercise price of $75 per share, the fair market value of a share of Employer stock at the time the option is granted. Employee may exercise the option only during employment with Employer or within 90 days after cessation of employment.
>
> On January 1 of Year 2, when the fair market value of 1,000 shares of Employer stock is $100,000, Employee exercises the option and purchases 1,000 shares of Employer stock in exchange for a nontransferable recourse note ("Note") secured by the stock Employee receives on the exercise of the option. The Note has a stated principal amount of $75,000, which is payable at maturity on December 31 of Year 11. The Note also provides for payments of interest on December 31 of each year the Note is outstanding. The interest rate is one-year LIBOR (determined as of January 1 of each year the Note is outstanding) plus 25 basis points. The interest rate on the Note is not less than the appropriate applicable Federal rate (AFR) on the date the Note is issued. The stock is not subject to a substantial risk of forfeiture within the meaning of § 83(c).
>
> In Year 2, Employee includes $25,000 as compensation income under § 83(a). Employer reports $25,000 of compensation income on the Form W-2 issued to Employee for Year 2 and claims a corresponding deduction in Year 2 under § 83(h).
>
> In Years 2 and 3, Employee makes the required interest payments under the Note. On January 1 of Year 4, the fair market value of the Employer stock has declined to $50,000 and Employer and Employee agree to reduce the stated principal amount of the Note from $75,000 to $50,000. The interest rate on the Note is not less than the appropriate AFR on the date the Note is modified.

The IRS ruled that the normal analysis under Treas. Reg. § 1.83-4(c) applies to this fact setting. Thus, cancellation of a portion of indebtedness—no matter what the reason—constitutes compensation. The use of a note does not change the original purchase price, and fluctuations in value go only to the ultimate capital gain or loss on the stock. Any subsequent reduction in the purchase price by the service recipient is simply additional compensation to the service provider—i.e., taxable as wages and thus also subject to payroll taxes. The IRS noted that the same rules apply to reduction in interest or a change in the terms of the note from recourse to nonrecourse.

CHAPTER 8

FINAL AND PROPOSED TAX REGULATIONS

Contents

1. Section 409A Deferred Compensation Rules 88
   Notice 2005-1 and proposed regulations under 409A:
   Specific application of the new rules to equity awards 88
   Overview of coverage 89
   General application of the new rules 89
   Specific application of the new rules to equity awards 90
   Valuation requirements for options and SARs 93
   Timeline for compliance 96
   2005 transition rules 96

2. Final Regulations for Statutory Stock Options 97
   Final statutory stock option regulations: Treasury Regulations
   Sections 1.421-424 97
   Final regulations for option transfers to related parties under
   Section 83 103

The first years of the twenty-first century have produced a steady stream of tax guidance that will have a significant and ongoing effect on equity compensation. Notable among this guidance are the proposed regulations to Section 409A of the Internal Revenue Code, which deal with the complex new rules related to deferred compensation. This lengthy set of proposed rules has already been through several incarnations since early 2005, and it is still in its comment period. Many kinks remain to be worked out. Equally important, but less confusing, are the final statutory stock option regulations (i.e., regulations under Sections 421–424 of the Code). These rules were years in the making and contained no surprises when they were finalized in 2004.

1. Section 409A Deferred Compensation Rules

With the American Jobs Creation Act of 2004, Congress added new Section 409A to the Code, thus adopting sweeping changes to the tax treatment of deferred compensation. Transition guidance to Section 409A was issued by the Internal Revenue Service (IRS) in Notice 2005-1 (December 2004, as revised in January 2005) (the "Transition Guidance"). The impetus for Section 409A came from perceived abuses of deferred compensation by top executives in large companies. Over the years, such companies had developed many techniques for all but guaranteeing deferred compensation payments (using trusts and similar vehicles) while still remaining within the technical rules exempting such funds from immediate taxation to the executive. In effect, these techniques provided executives with interest-free loans of the tax money that would otherwise have been due, while at the same time postponing the company's tax deduction (until actual payment) and making the fund assets unavailable to the company in the interim.

Under the new law, those halcyon days of discretionary deferrals are essentially over. As of January 1, 2005, any compensation deferred under a "nonqualified deferred compensation plan" (NDCP) will be currently taxable unless it is subject to a substantial risk of forfeiture (i.e., using the principles of Section 83 of the Code) or satisfies the rigorous requirements of Section 409A, which are summarized below.

Notice 2005-1 and proposed regulations under 409A: Specific application of the new rules to equity awards

As we have noted, many equity and equity-based awards are exempted from the Section 409A definition of NDCP, either as a result of the statutory language or under the regulatory guidance described below. In Notice 2005-1, "Guidance Under Section 409A of the Internal Revenue Code," the IRS provided initial guidance on how Section 409A applies to stock appreciation rights, restricted stock, and nonstatutory stock options granted after October 3, 2004. Note that awards granted before that date that were earned and vested as of December 31, 2004, are exempt from Section 409A regardless of their terms (so long as such terms are not materially modified after October 3, 2004). On September 29, 2005, the IRS issued proposed regulations under Section 409A, with further elaboration in Notice 2006-4, which was actually issued in 2005.

The proposed regulations are 238 pages long and cover all aspects of Section 409A, not just those dealing with equity compensation. We do not provide a summary of that other material here. While the proposed regulations laid out the basic framework, subsequent IRS pronouncements have added further detail and clarification, and more will be added in 2006. Therefore, users of this document should be sure to read it in the context of recent developments.

Overview of coverage

As of January 1, 2005, any compensation deferred under a "nonqualified deferred compensation plan" (NDCP) is currently taxable unless it is subject to a substantial risk of forfeiture (i.e., using the principles of Section 83 of the Code) or satisfies the rigorous requirements of Section 409A summarized below. For purposes of Section 409A, nonqualified deferred compensation generally does *not* include: (1) qualified benefit plans, such as ESOPs or 401(k) plans; (2) sick leave, death benefits, or similar arrangements; (3) statutory stock options (i.e., ISOs and Section 423 ESPPs); (4) NSOs granted at fair market value (subject to certain limitations); (5) restricted stock awards with no additional deferral features; and (6) non-discounted stock appreciation rights (SARs). All other forms of nonqualified deferred compensation can be assumed to be deferred under a NDCP, *including*: (1) nonqualified ESPPs that include a discount feature; (2) nonstatutory options and SARs that include a deferral feature (i.e., allowing an employee to defer receipt of the award after it has already been exercised); and (3) phantom stock, restricted stock units, performance shares, and similar plans.

General application of the new rules

If compensation deferred under a NDCP is not otherwise subject to a substantial risk of forfeiture, it will be taxed at the time of deferral unless the following conditions are satisfied:

1. The initial election to defer (including form of payment) is made before the start of the year in which the compensation is earned. An

election to defer "performance-based" compensation may be made up to six months before the end of the performance period.

2. Any additional elections must be made at least 12 months before the date the deferred compensation would otherwise have been received, and in most cases deferral must be for at least five years after the original payment date.

3. Distributions may be permitted only upon separation from service (for certain "key employees" of public companies, this includes a six-month waiting period); at a specified date or dates (under a fixed schedule); or upon disability, death, change in control, and unforeseeable emergency, in each case as such terms are defined by Section 409A and its regulations.

4. No acceleration of payments is permissible, except as the IRS may provide in future regulations.

Note that short-term deferrals (i.e., no later than two and one-half months after the close of the year the substantial risk of forfeiture lapses) will not run afoul of Section 409A.

Section 409A and the Section 409A rules are extremely complicated. Many issues (including issues affecting stock options) remain to be resolved during the regulatory process and in years to come. Failure to comply with these rules triggers severe and adverse tax consequences. As noted above, the participant's total deferrals under the NDCP are immediately taxed as income except to the extent not subject to a substantial risk of forfeiture (and not previously taxed). In addition, there is a 20% penalty tax on the amount of the deferral and any earnings attributable to it, plus cumulative interest at the underpayment rate, plus 1% on the tax that should have been paid on the original deferral and any related earnings.

Specific application of the new rules to equity awards

Many types of equity and equity-based awards are exempted from the Section 409A definition of NDCP, either as a result of the statutory language or the Section 409A rules. The following discussion summarizes the IRS interpretation of Section 409A as it applies to SARs, restricted stock, and NSOs granted after October 3, 2004. Note that awards granted before that date that were earned and vested as of December 31, 2004, are exempt from Section 409A regardless of their terms (so long as such terms are not materially modified after October 3, 2004).

Nonqualified stock options (NSOs) and stock appreciation rights (SARs)

The Section 409A rules clarify that both NSOs and SARs (collectively, "stock rights") will be exempt from Section 409A so long as (1) the exercise price can never be less than the fair market value of the underlying stock on the date of grant; (2) the stock right is exercisable for "service recipient" stock; (3) the stock right includes no deferral features other than deferral of income until exercise; and (4) the stock right is not modified in a way that would otherwise subject it to Section 409A. As with the other exempt forms of compensation, stock rights may be thrown into the purview of Section 409A if they are coupled with features that would otherwise be classified as payments under a NDCP. Note that generally, NSOs transferred in a merger or acquisition will not trigger deferred compensation treatment if they meet the 2004 statutory option regulations governing transfer of statutory options in a corporate transaction.

For purposes of setting the exercise price, Section 409A provides that fair market value may be determined using "any reasonable valuation method," and the proposed regulations elaborate on this concept. With publicly traded companies, this is never a problem. However, with the stakes now raised for stock rights, privately held companies must pay special attention to the hurdles inherent in setting fair market value so as to avoid inadvertently granting NSOs or SARs at a discount. This is discussed in more detail below.

Restricted stock

Generally, grants of restricted stock (whether or not unvested at grant) will be subject to Section 83 of the Code rather than to Section 409A. However, the Section 409A rules note that a plan under which a service provider obtains a legally binding right to receive property in a future year may provide for the deferral of compensation and thus become a

NDCP. A restricted stock unit, for example, will fall into Section 409A and accordingly must satisfy the general requirements to avoid early taxation (i.e., no deferral of delivery after vesting).

Modifications

If an award's terms are changed to offer an additional deferral feature—such as an extension of the time to exercise after employment terminates—the award becomes subject to Section 409A, although it is not yet clear how those awards will be valued for tax purposes. In contrast, plan changes that allow different forms of payment, such as the addition of a cashless exercise feature, do not constitute modifications that make an award subject to Section 409A (although they may be considered modifications for other purposes, such as compliance with the tax rules governing ISOs).

Discounted stock options or SARs subject to Section 409A that were not fully vested as of the end of 2004 can be modified up to the end of 2006 can be replaced with stock options or SARs that meet the rules. Additionally, new payment deadlines can be instituted within this time frame to provide either that SARs or options have a fixed exercise date or dates, or that the award recipient can specify a date or dates.

Business combinations

The option issuer may own as little as 20% of the service recipient company so long as the use of that company's stock has a legitimate business purpose. If a service provider works for a closely held subsidiary of a public company, only the public company's stock is the service recipient stock.

Performance vesting

Stock options and SARs subject to Section 409A may vest based on performance criteria so long as the performance period is at least one year and the compensation is based solely on appreciation of the value of the stock. The performance criteria can be determined up to 90 days after the grant. Criteria can be subjective, but the more specific they are, the less likely they are to run afoul of the rules.

Stock appreciation rights

The prior regulations subjected all SARs in closely held companies, and cash-settled SARs of public companies, to Section 409A. Provided certain basic requirements are met, SARs will now be excluded from coverage. The most significant of these requirements is that SARs be issued at a reasonably determined fair market value, as described in detail below. SARs, like options, may not provide for deferrals beyond the date at which the award vests and is exercised. Payments for the award cannot exceed the difference between the fair market value at grant and exercise.

Valuation requirements for options and SARs

To avoid coverage under the Section 409A rules, valuations for SARs and NSOs in closely held companies will need to adhere to more rigorous standards than is currently the norm. Public companies can use the trading price using the first or last price on the day the grant is awarded, an average over the 30 days before or after, or any other reasonable method consistently applied. Closely held companies, however, will have to follow stricter rules, as further explored below.

As proposed, the Section 409A rules set forth three alternatives for closely held companies. Such issuers have a choice of:

- Following the established standards for ESOP valuations;
- Using a formula valuation that establishes fair market valuation for purposes of Treas. Reg. § 1.83-5 *and* that is used on a consistent basis for other transactions; or
- If in business less than 10 years, using a formula valuation that meets somewhat (but not much) less rigorous guidelines.

In each, the valuation method must be used consistently with respect to any obligation of the employer with respect to the class of shares involved.

ESOP valuation standards

Under the new rules, companies with ESOPs may simply use their existing valuations. Companies without ESOPs, however, may also consider adopting this approach. ESOP rules require an independent, outside appraisal performed at least annually. The appraiser must be a qualified professional with no other business relationship to the company. The appraisals must determine what a willing buyer would pay a willing seller for the company. Specific rules were never adopted on how to conduct an appraisal, but a consensus has developed in the industry that asset value, comparable companies, and (usually most importantly) capitalization of future earnings should all be weighed. Once an enterprise value is established, appropriate discounts for whether the securities represent a control interest and a lack of marketability must be applied.

Treasury Regulations Section 1.83-5 formula valuations

Treas. Reg. § 1.83-5 sets out rules for setting the value of property subject to a "nonlapse restriction," i.e., a restriction on the acquisition or sale of the property that is not subject to subsequent change (such as a NQSO with time-based vesting that is subsequently modified, making it a new grant for Section 409A purposes), as follows:

> If stock in a corporation is subject to a nonlapse restriction which requires the transferee to sell such stock only at a formula price based on book value, a reasonable multiple of earnings or a reasonable combination thereof, the price so determined will ordinarily be regarded as determinative of the fair market value of such property for purposes of section 83. However, in certain circumstances the formula price will not be considered to be the fair market value of property subject to such a formula price restriction, even though the formula price restriction is a substantial factor in determining such value. For example, where the formula price is the current book value of stock, the book value of the stock at some time in the future may be a more accurate measure of the value of the stock than the current book value of the stock for purposes of determining the fair market value of the stock at the time the stock becomes substantially vested.

In other words, the formula must be more than formulaic—it must consider what approach most closely resembles reasonable fair market value. The Section 409A rules add to this the requirement that the same formula must be used for any nonlapse restrictions applicable to the transfer of shares of that class of shares, and that that it be used for any noncompensatory purpose involving that class of stock, such as regulatory filings, loan covenants, issuances and repurchases of stock from non-service providers, and so on. This rule also does not apply if the award is paid in stock and the stock is transferable without a nonlapse restriction. A key element here is that if the safe harbor is satisfied, the burden of proof is on the IRS to demonstrate the unreasonableness of the valuation method, rather than on the company to show the reasonableness of the method.

Start-up company valuations

Issuers in business for less than 10 years are eligible to use a written valuation made "reasonably and in good faith" that takes into account relevant business factors and is performed by "a person or persons with significant knowledge and experience or training in performing significant valuations." The company must not reasonably anticipate a change of control or IPO in the next 12 months and must have no class of tradable securities. The company's stock must not be subject to any put or call right.

General issues in determining reasonableness

Any valuation needs to consider at least several factors, including the present value of future cash flows; asset value; comparable company valuations and relevant ratios (such as price to earnings); any prior sales of stock; consistent application of the value, premiums, and discounts for factors such as control, lack of marketability, and so on; and the relevance of other valuations performed for different purposes. Valuations that are not current (do not use information from the prior 12 months) are not considered reasonable.

In further guidance issued in Notice 2006-4 (Dec. 29, 2005), the IRS announced that as an interim measure under Section 409A, issuers may adopt any reasonable method for establishing fair market value for awards issued before January 1, 2005. For awards issued after that date, but before the effective date of the proposed regulations (January 1, 2007), issuers may rely on the guidance in the proposed regulations. Other reasonable methods may also be acceptable if satisfactory to the IRS, provided that such methods (at a minimum) reflect information updated for the last 12 months, be used consistently for other purposes, and take into account all relevant information available to the company. For awards issued after January 1, 2007, companies must rely on the proposed regulations, but the IRS noted that it may yet issue further guidance on their implementation.

Timeline for compliance

Companies have until December 31, 2006, to amend their plans to comply with Section 409A. However, between January 1, 2005, and December 31, 2006, plans must operate in good-faith compliance, which can be demonstrated by following the proposed regulations or the preliminary guidance contained in Notice 2005-1. Plans may be amended to provide for new payment elections as long as any deferral elections are made no later than December 31, 2006. Both of these deadlines represent a one-year extension of deadlines stated in Notice 2005-1.

Awards that were earned and vested before the end of 2004 are not subject to Section 409A, but those that were exercisable but unvested before that date are subject to these rules. Amounts deferred before December 31, 2004, are covered by the rules if they were made under a plan that was materially modified after October 3, 2004. The Section 409A rules allow for evergreen deferral elections that occur regularly.

2005 transition rules

The Transition Guidance set out special rules for equity grants made before December 31, 2005:

> [P]rovided that the cancellation and reissuance [of a stock option or stock appreciation right] occurs on or before December 31, 2005, it will not be a material modification to replace a stock option or stock appreciation right otherwise providing for a deferral of compensation. The preceding sentence only applies if (i) the number of shares which form the basis of the new stock option or new stock appreciation right corresponds directly to the number of shares subject to the original stock option or stock appreciation right; and (ii) the new stock option or new stock appreciation right does not provide any additional benefit to the service recipient (other than the benefit directly due to a change in form of the award to a form not treated as a deferral of compensation). A replacement stock option or replacement stock appreciation right will be treated as meeting the requirements of clause (i) of the preceding sentence if the new grant is

made in accordance with the principles of § 1.424-1(a)(5) except to the extent necessary to ensure that the new grant does not violate § 409A.

In other words, an NSO with a discounted exercise price could be amended to increase the exercise price to equal to fair market value at grant. Similarly, a cash-only SAR could be converted to a stock option or S-SAR that, based on its terms, would be excluded from the definition of deferral of compensation.

2. Final Regulations for Statutory Stock Options

The final comprehensive rewrite of rules for ISOs and Section 423 ESPP options was effective as of August 3, 2004. While the rules provided no major departures from existing procedures, they did codify existing practices and clarify several uncertainties over issues such as how awards are treated in mergers, calculating the $100,00 rule, wash sales, shareholder approval requirements, and other matters. On the $100,000 rule, the IRS issued somewhat ambiguous guidelines on how to value shares in closely held companies, an issue that (as noted above) was revisited in more detail in conjunction with the Section 409A proposed regulations. In addition, the IRS published its final regulations governing transfers of compensatory stock options between optionees and related persons under Section 83 of the Code.

Final statutory stock option regulations: Treasury Regulations Sections 1.421-424

In proposed regulations published June 9, 2003 (26 CFR Parts 1 and 14a, Reg-112917-02, June 9, 2003), the IRS proposed an update, reorganization, and elaboration of existing rules governing statutory stock options (i.e., ISOs and ESPP options). Final regulations went into effect on August 3, 2004. The final regulations do not make dramatic changes to the proposed regulations, although a number of technical uncertainties have been resolved. The final regulations replaced those existing since February 7, 1984. Generally, the rules went effective August 3, 2004, with some limited grandfathering permitted for options granted before June

9, 2003. As of this writing (June 2006), all statutory stock options are subject to the final regulations.

The regulations are very detailed and cover a variety of issues, but most simply restate, reorganize, and renumber existing regulations. The following summarizes the significant substantive changes:

Section 83(b) elections

Under Section 83 of the Code, the optionee must pay ordinary income tax on the difference between the purchase price and the fair market value of the shares (the "spread") on the later of the date of exercise or the date of vesting. The Section 83(b) election is a technical device that allows the optionee to gamble that the spread will be greater on the date of vesting than on the date of exercise. Filing the election within 30 days of exercise "freezes" the spread and limits the optionee's ordinary income tax to the value at the date of exercise. Any additional gain is treated as capital gain (and any loss is a capital loss).

As a general rule, ISOs are not subject to Section 83. However, there are two situations where Section 83 might apply to an ISO that is exercised for unvested stock: (1) if the ISO is later disqualified and thus becomes an NSO, and (2) for purposes of computing the alternative minimum tax (AMT). To anticipate the disqualification situation, practitioners sometimes suggested that optionees file a "prophylactic Section 83(b) election" when exercising an ISO for unvested shares. The theory was that at the time of a disqualification, the taxpayer could take the position that an 83(b) election to freeze the spread had already been filed, and thus his or her ordinary income would be limited to the spread at exercise. The final regulations reject the use of the prophylactic 83(b) election for ISOs.

In the second situation, the optionee files a Section 83(b) election for AMT purposes only—i.e., to freeze the gain includible in the AMT computation to the spread on exercise. This makes sense because for AMT purposes, an ISO is treated as if it were an NSO. The final regulations permit taxpayers to use a Section 83(b) election for AMT.

$100,000 rule

One of the rules for an incentive stock option is that not more than $100,000 in options, measured by taking the number of options times the fair market value of the stock at grant, can first become exercisable in any one year. The regulations expand on and incorporate IRS Notice 87-49 on this issue. For purposes of the rule, options are taken into account in the order they are issued. Options that are not ISOs when issued are disregarded. "First exercisable" is defined to mean the calendar year in which the option can first be exercised (normally, but not always, the year of vesting). This can get tricky if there is a change of control trigger or performance trigger that allows exercise if a change of control occurs before vesting or disallows exercise until a performance target is met. Under the regulations, if there is such an acceleration provision, then options first exercised during a calendar year pursuant to an acceleration clause do not affect the application of the $100,000 rule for options exercised before the acceleration provision. All of these prior options can be exercised, up to the $100,000 limit, even if the accelerated options are exercised in the same year. However, any options from the accelerated group that are in excess of $100,000 minus the fair market value at grant of the previously exercised options that year are disqualified as ISOs. For instance, if an employee has options with a fair market value of $75,000 at grant that first become exercisable in 2007, and options with a fair market value at grant of $50,000 that accelerate in the same year, the first group of options is considered an ISO in its entirety. The second group is bifurcated, with $25,000 being an ISO and $25,000 an NSO. If a company bifurcates an option into an ISO and NSO to meet the $100,000 rule, it can issue a separate certificate for the ISO or designate it an ISO in plan records and not have this considered a modification of the plan.

The regulations provide that an option is "disregarded for purposes of the $100,000 limit if, prior to the calendar year during which it would otherwise become exercisable for the first time, the option is modified and thereafter ceases to be an incentive stock option." Similar treatment applies to an ISO that is disqualified by being transferred or cancelled. Otherwise, modified, transferred, or cancelled options are considered outstanding until the end of the calendar year during which these awards would be first exercisable. Disqualifying dispositions also have no effect on the $100,000 determination.

Note that Treas. Reg. § 1.422-3(e) states that calculation of fair market value for these purposes may be made by any "reasonable method," including independent appraisals and valuation in accordance with the gift tax rules.

Brokerage fees

An optionee who disqualifies an ISO by selling underlying shares before the end of the statutory holding period must pay ordinary income tax on the spread at exercise or the gain on sale, whichever is less. In the past, companies have reduced net income for optionees by deducting brokerage fees from the reportable spread; the final regulations disallow such deductions.

Corporate consolidations

Under the final regulations, the requirement for shareholder approval of the plan will be satisfied in a corporate consolidation if the merger agreement fully describes the assumption of the plan. Separate shareholder approval will not be required for assumption or substitution of statutory options in connection with a merger if such options were already granted under an approved plan.

Definition of "employee"

In the case of an assumption or substitution of an ISO, an option will be treated as granted to an employee if the optionee is in the three-month period following employment, as well as to currently employed individuals. Optionees on leave pursuant to a statute (such as the Family Medical Leave Act) or contract that provides for continuing rights of reemployment continue to be considered employees for these purposes.

Definition of "corporation"

Corporations are now defined to include not just C corporations but also any entity choosing to be taxed as a corporation under federal income tax rules, including S corporations, foreign corporations, and limited liability corporations (LLCs). Corporations electing to be taxed as partnerships, including LLCs, limited liability partnerships, and limited partnerships, would not be defined as a corporation. This definition makes it clear, for instance, that an employee of an LLC taxed as a corporation can receive a statutory option.

Definition of "option"

The definition of an option is expanded to include warrants if the warrants meet other qualifications of the regulations. Warrants, like options, are financial instruments allowing the purchaser to buy shares at a fixed price for a defined period of time. Warrants are not usually issued specifically in return for service to the employer and usually carry a price at grant or purchase greater than fair market value. If a warrant otherwise meets the rules for an incentive option, the regulations would allow it to be defined as an option.

Definition of "stock"

Stock is defined to include capital stock of any class and with any combination of voting rights or no voting rights. Preferred stock and special classes of stock authorized only to be issued to employees also qualify (tracking stock in a division issued just to employees, for instance, would presumably be an example of this), provided that this stock has the same rights and characteristics of capital stock.

Electronic forms allowed

Existing rules require options and option plans to be in writing; the new regulations allow electronic forms to be used as well, provided they meet regulatory requirements for such forms.

Maximum number of shares

Code Section 422(b)(1) requires that companies provide shareholders with information about the total number of shares subject to option under an ISO plan. The new regulations clarify that this requirement applies for purposes of ISOs only. Companies may meet the requirement in a variety of ways, including by (1) a number certain, (2) a percentage of shares outstanding at the date of adoption, and (3) an increase in shares relative to the number of shares outstanding based on a defined ratio. Note that for purposes of share counting, if outstanding shares are used to exercise an option, only the net number of shares issued to the optionee after the exercise is considered for purposes of calculating the maximum number of shares.

Modification of options

Under Code Section 424(h)(1), modifications, extensions, and renewals of options are treated as the grant of a new option. Generally, an option will be "modified" only if the change results in an increase in benefits to the optionee. The final regulations reiterate that a change in option terms by virtue of a "corporate transaction" will not be treated as a modification for these purposes. "Corporate transactions" include mergers, consolidations, reorganizations, and liquidations; changes in the corporate name; and other changes as may be prescribed by the Commissioner. Stock splits and dividends will not be modifications so long as they are proportionate and do not result in more than minor changes to the value of the awards. The final regulations eliminate the earlier requirement that the transaction result in a significant number of employees "being transferred to a new employer or discharged or in the creation or severance of a parent-subsidiary relationship."

Certain exercises of discretion will not be treated as modifications so long as such discretion has been previously authorized, including the exercise of corporate discretion to (1) modify an option with respect to the payment of employment or withholding taxes and (2) pay a bonus, make a loan, or offer the right to tender previously owned stock when an option is exercised. Note that if such discretion has not been previously authorized, the exercise of such discretion will be treated as a modification.

Shareholder approval

In general, shareholder approval for statutory options is required if there is a change in the aggregate number of shares or in the employees (or class or classes of employees) eligible for the options. The final regulations expand on these issues and specifically include situations in which a change in the shares to which the option applies, as well as a change in the issuing corporation. For instance, if a plan provides that a subsidiary's employees receive statutory options in the subsidiary and it is subsequently amended to permit grants from the parent, shareholder approval will be required within 12 months of the amendment. As noted above, additional shareholder approval is not required for validly granted ISOs assumed in a corporate transaction.

One final point with regard to shareholder approval: the final regulations provide that an ISO plan adopted by the board of directors "subject to shareholder approval" *will be adopted on the date the plan is approved by shareholders.* If the board of directors stipulates a condition for adoption, the deemed adoption date is when that condition is satisfied. The final regulations raise issues, yet to be resolved, as to whether ISO grants made before shareholder approval will ever be valid. Note that this rule does not apply to Section 423 ESPPs.

Treatment of transferred options

This has been an area of some uncertainty for some time. Under the final regulations, an option that is transferred to a trust in a manner such that the option holder is considered the beneficiary of the trust still qualifies as a statutory option. Options transferred pursuant to a divorce, however, now lose their status as statutory options as of the date of transfer.

Wash sales

On a disqualifying disposition of an ISO, the optionee pays ordinary income tax on the lesser of the spread at exercise or the actual gain on sale. In a declining market, such a disqualification could offer a better tax benefit than holding for the full statutory holding period: e.g., if the spread on exercise were $100 and the gain on sale were only $50, it might be better to sell and pay tax on $50 than hold and pay AMT on $100. A recent strategy to take advantage of this anomalous result was to sell in a disqualification, pay ordinary income tax on the gain, and then get back into the market shortly thereafter. The new regulations clarify that this transaction qualifies as a "wash sale" under Section 1091 of the Code. Accordingly, the sale is treated as never having occurred, and the optionee will be required to pay tax on the full spread at exercise (in the example, $100).

Final regulations for option transfers to related parties under Section 83

The IRS published final regulations governing transfers of compensatory stock options between optionees and related persons under Section 83 of the Code (T.D. 9148, Aug. 10, 2004). New Treas. Reg. § 1.83-7 excludes certain family members and control group members from favorable tax treatment under the "arm's length disposition" rules otherwise set out in the regulations to Section 83 after July 2, 2003.

In general, Section 83 permits a taxpayer who disposes of an option to a third party to close the compensatory portion of the transaction at the time of transfer rather than at the time of exercise. Treas. Reg. § 1.83-7 is intended to address a tax avoidance scheme that allowed optionees to take advantage of the arm's length disposition rules for options while still retaining control of the ultimate exercise. Under the terms of the scheme, the optionee would sell an unexercised NSO to a relative or family limited partnership in which the optionee had a substantial interest (and implicit control). In exchange, the optionee accepted a long-term unsecured note that would come due only when the buyer exercised the option and sold the stock. This resulted in no tax to the optionee until the note was paid off, and no tax (or note payments) to the buyer until the stock was sold. In essence, the transaction created ISO deferral treatment for an NSO, minus the alternative minimum tax problem.

For an extensive discussion of the IRS's view on Treas. Reg. § 1.83-7, see its Coordinated Issues Paper titled "Transfer or Sale of Compensatory Stock Options or Restricted Stock to Unrelated Persons," effective October 15, 2004, and posted on the IRS Web site at *www.irs.gov/pub/irs-utl/compensatory_final.pdf.*

CHAPTER 9

Securities Law Legislation and Rulings

Contents

1. **The Sarbanes-Oxley Act of 2002** 106
   Prohibition on personal loans to directors and executive officers 106
   Accelerated Section 16 filing deadlines 109
   Foreign private issuers 110
   SEC rulemaking 110
   Recommendations 112
   Forfeiture of compensation and stock sale profits by CEOs and CFOs upon restatements due to misconduct 113
   Freeze on extraordinary payments to directors and officers 114

2. **SEC Rulings and No-Action Letters** 114
   Accounting issues 115
   Plan operations 117
   Registration exemptions 120
   Reporting and disclosure issues 121
   Shareholder rights 122
   Stock exchange rulings 130

The Sarbanes-Oxley Act of 2002 ("Sarbanes-Oxley" or the "2002 Act") made far-reaching changes in federal rules applicable to corporate America and its executives, auditors, and advisers. In addition to corporate governance and accounting reforms, the 2002 Act had an immediate effect on many executive and equity compensation arrangements (including stock benefit plans) and their administration.

As of this writing, the repercussions of the 2002 Act are continuing to be absorbed by the legal, corporate and investor community. Securities and Exchange Commission (SEC) No-Action Rulings reflect some of the changes (and confusion). In early 2006, issues relating to executive compensation and governance—particularly with respect to stock option granting—were at center stage. We expect to see many important issues arise as the community's experience with the new rules continues to develop.

1. The Sarbanes-Oxley Act of 2002[1]
By William R. Pomierski and William J. Quinlan, Jr.

The Sarbanes-Oxley Act of 2002 created a comprehensive reform of corporate governance and accounting rules. Directors, executives, Section 16 compliance officers, and human resources administrators will want to consider closely the following provisions under the 2002 Act:

- Prohibition on personal loans to directors and executive officers
- Accelerated Section 16 filing deadlines
- Restrictions on stock transactions during retirement plan blackout periods
- Forfeiture of executive pay due to accounting restatements
- Freeze on extraordinary payments to directors and officers

Prohibition on personal loans to directors and executive officers

Section 402 of the 2002 Act amends Section 13 of the Securities Exchange Act of 1934 (the "1934 Act") to prohibit publicly held U.S. and non-U.S. companies from making or extending personal loans to directors and executive officers. Section 402 became effective on July 30, 2002, subject to grandfathering provisions and certain limited exceptions.

---

1. This part of the chapter was taken, with minor additions, from Appendix A of William R. Pomierski and William J. Quinlan, Jr., "Federal Securities Law Considerations for Incentive Stock Plans," chapter 2 in *Selected Issues in Equity Compensation,* 3rd ed. (NCEO, 2006).

General loan prohibition under Section 402

Section 402 states that "[i]t shall be unlawful for any issuer (as defined in Section 2 of the Sarbanes-Oxley Act of 2002), directly or indirectly, including through any subsidiary, to extend or maintain credit, to arrange for the extension of credit, or to renew an extension of credit, in the form of a personal loan to or for any director or executive officer (or equivalent thereof) of that issuer." Unless grandfathering treatment or an exception applies, effective July 30, 2002, issuers are prohibited from extending a personal loan in any manner to a director or executive officer.

Directors and executive officers

The term "director" is defined in Section 3(a)(7) of the 1934 Act as "any director of a corporation or any person performing similar functions with respect to any organization, whether incorporated or unincorporated." There are real questions about advisory, emeritus, or honorary directors, and the SEC interpretations under Section 16 of the 1934 Act may be relevant to this issue. The SEC has indicated in various releases that it believes that advisory and emeritus directors generally should be treated as directors for Section 16 purposes, but that honorary directors should not be so treated.

As noted above, the provisions of Section 402 of the 2002 Act are implemented as an amendment to the 1934 Act. Accordingly, unless and until the SEC adopts a different definition, the term "executive officer" under Section 402 should be interpreted in a manner consistent with existing SEC rules. 1934 Act Rule 3b-7 defines an "executive officer" (for purposes of, among others, proxy, 10-K, and other 1934 Act disclosures) as the "president, any vice president of the registrant in charge of a principal business unit, division or function (such as sales, administration or finance), any other officer who performs a policy making function or any other person who performs similar policy making functions for the registrant." Executive officers of subsidiaries may be deemed executive officers of a publicly held company if they perform policy-making functions for the publicly held company.

Grandfather protection

A limited grandfather provision provides some relief but raises many questions. Section 402 exempts loans maintained before July 30, 2002, "provided that there is no material modification to any term of any such extension of credit or any renewal of any such extension of credit" on or after July 30, 2002. A material modification of any term results in loss of grandfather treatment. Any action that might be considered to be a change to the terms of a loan should be carefully considered, given that Section 402 may be violated even if the change is minor and does not affect the overall financing arrangement.

Identifying transactions potentially subject to Section 402

The ambiguity as to what is a "personal loan" and the breadth of what may be considered an arrangement for "extension of credit" suggest that publicly held companies should immediately identify all transactions potentially subject to Section 402. Common arrangements that may be viewed to involve an extension of credit are split-dollar life insurance and cashless stock option exercises. The following is a partial list of other transactions with directors and executives officers that may be treated as an extension of credit:

- Loans to purchase stock, a personal residence, or other property
- Loans to meet margin calls upon a decline in the price of the company's stock
- Loans for relocation to a different geographic area
- Routine advances for business purposes (such as reimbursement accounts and travel expense allowances), particularly if repaid over long period of time
- Personal use of company credit cards
- Indemnification payments made under company bylaws or an employment agreement before a determination of entitlement to such payment
- Use of company funds to meet an executive's payroll tax obligations for nonqualified deferred compensation benefits
- Signing bonuses subject to repayment on early termination of employment

Cashless stock option exercises under Section 402

A common executive compensation practice that has been affected by Section 402 is the cashless exercise of stock options facilitated through a broker. In a cashless exercise, the option holder instructs a brokerage firm to sell a sufficient number of the shares being acquired by the option exercise to satisfy the option price and any applicable withholding taxes. The broker sells the shares and remits the exercise price and any taxes required to be withheld to the company, with any balance remitted to the option holder. The company delivers the requisite number of shares to the broker and the balance to the option holder.

There are two common methods to execute a cashless exercise of a stock option. A broker may sell the shares on the date of receipt of exercise instructions and remit the exercise price and withholding taxes to the company a few days later, on the date of the settlement of the sale of those shares. Alternatively, a broker may sell the shares on the date of receipt of the instructions and remit the exercise price and withholding taxes immediately to the company, treating the amount as a margin loan to the option holder. Other variations on this practice also exist.

Any of these cashless exercise methods may be viewed as resulting in an "extension of credit" under Section 402. A broker-assisted direct sale involves the company making stock or cash available to the option holder for the exercise, albeit only for a very short period of time. While a margin loan from a broker does not involve the use of the company funds, it may also be subject to Section 402 to the extent that the company is viewed as having "arranged" this financing by establishing the cashless exercise program with the brokerage firm. None of these methods would seem to be the type of loan targeted by the Congress under the 2002 Act. It was hoped that the SEC would issue guidance to clarify the impact of Section 402 on cashless exercise programs, but the SEC has not done so to date (but it has also not objected to the continuing use of the practice). The margin loan method discussed above has become an acceptable practice to avoid Section 402 problems.

Accelerated Section 16 filing deadlines

Section 403 of the 2002 Act amended Section 16(a) of the 1934 Act to require Section 16 reporting persons (directors, 10% or more shareholders, and certain executive officers) to report changes in beneficial ownership of issuer securities within two business days. The two-day filing requirement became effective August 29, 2002, under amended Section 16 rules adopted by the SEC on August 27, 2002 (SEC Release No. 34-46421).

This rule took on special significance with the backdating scandals that emerged in 2006. A number of companies claimed that their options were issued on dates that, upon examination, turned out to coincide with an unusual pattern of low stock prices. The scandal, of course, was that the awards apparently had been issued later, but backdated. Under the old rules, companies had to report any option grants within 45 days of the grant, making it easier to backdate (albeit still raising a host of other issues about advisability and legality outside the reporting aspect of securities laws). Under Sarbanes-Oxley, grants must be reported within two days.

The 2002 Act also requires the SEC to adopt rules requiring that Section 16(a) reports be filed electronically (rather than in paper form) no later than July 30, 2003. These rules went into effect on June 30, 2003. To file electronically, SEC rules require each Section 16 reporting person to apply for and obtain his or her own access codes to the SEC's Electronic Data Gathering, Analysis and Retrieval System (EDGAR).

Foreign private issuers

Currently, foreign private issuers with securities registered under the Exchange Act are not subject to any aspect of Section 16. The SEC has indicated that it does not intend to change the exemption for foreign private issuers.

SEC rulemaking

Highlights of the revised Section 16 reporting rules are follows:

- All transactions occurring on or after August 29, 2002, must be reported on a Form 4 received by the SEC no later than 10:00 p.m. Eastern time on the second business day following the transaction date except as set forth below. These include:
    — Option grants and exercises
    — Stock awards, performance share awards, and SARs

- Option repricings, cancellations, regrants, and amendments
- Dispositions to the issuer, including stock swaps and share withholding to pay taxes
- Open market purchases and sales

• All of the reporting deferrals for transactions between the issuer and Section 16 reporting persons set forth in Rule 16b-3 will be subject to two-business day reporting on Form 4 except for the following:
  - Routine purchases under the payroll deduction provisions of a 401(k) plan (including an excess benefit plan), employee stock purchase plan, or employee stock ownership plan (ESOP), which transactions remain exempt from reporting (but must be included in the shares beneficially owned column).
  - "Discretionary transactions" under 401(k) and other employee benefit plans and certain transactions made pursuant to so-called Rule 10b5-1 plans, which transactions must be reported on a Form 4 under a special "deemed execution" rule discussed below, which can allow up to five-business day reporting.

• All of the exemptions contained in the Section 16(a) rules remain in effect and may either be voluntarily reported on a Form 4 at any time up to the due date of the Form 5 or reported on a Form 5 within 45 days of the end of the issuer's fiscal year. These include:
  - Gifts
  - Expiration of options without consideration
  - Small acquisitions, but not from the issuer or an employee benefit plan sponsored by the issuer
  - Stock splits and stock dividends
  - Pro-rata distributions
  - Transfers under domestic relations orders
  - Changes in form of beneficial ownership
  - Regular dividend reinvestment plan contributions

• The SEC has adopted special limited deferred reporting rules (up to five business days depending upon circumstances) for the following transactions:

- Transactions pursuant to a contract, instruction, or written plan for the purchase or sale of issuer equity securities that satisfies the affirmative defense conditions of Rule 10b5-1(c) where the Section 16 reporting person does not select the date(s) of execution (such as the first date of each month).
- Discretionary transactions where the Section 16 reporting person does not select the date(s) of execution.
- Deferred compensation plan investments in a company stock fund, but only if they fall within the scope of a Rule 10b5-1 plan.
- Transactions that occur over more than one day, but only if they fall within the scope of a Rule 10b5-1 plan.

The above transactions are subject to reporting on Form 4 within two business days of the "deemed execution" date of the transaction. The deemed execution date of the transaction will be the earlier of (1) the date on which the executing broker, dealer, or plan administrator notifies the Section 16 reporting person of the execution of the transaction, and (2) the third business day following the trade date. (The SEC noted in its release adopting the new rules that a trade confirmation sent through the mail could take several days to arrive and the SEC would, therefore, usually expect brokers, dealers, and plan administrators to provide the information needed for Section 16(a) reporting purposes to the Section 16 reporting person either electronically or by telephone.)

- The rules with respect to the timing of the filing of Form 3 (initial statement of beneficial ownership) have not changed. For a company that is already public, the Form 3 must be filed within 10 days of the person becoming a Section 16 reporting person. For companies going public, the Form 3 must be filed before the company goes public. The SEC noted that a transaction might be required to be filed on Form 4 before the due date of Form 3. In this situation, the SEC encouraged the filing of both the Form 3 and the Form 4 by the due date of the Form 4.

Recommendations

The following recommendations should be considered in order to comply with the revised Section 16 rules:

- Have a mandatory pre-clearance policy for all transactions as to which the timing is within the control of the Section 16 reporting person.

- For transactions as to which timing is outside the control of the Section 16 reporting person, require brokerage firms conducting transactions for the Section 16 reporting person to provide promptly upon trade execution, and certainly by the third business day, the information needed for Section 16(a) reporting purposes to the Section 16 reporting person either electronically or by telephone.

- Review and update the procedures for discretionary transactions under benefit plans to ensure that the Section 16 reporting person receives timely notification (no later than three business days) of execution of the transaction from the plan administrator.

- Educate all Section 16 reporting persons by a memorandum that they should read, sign, and return.

- Establish a cashless exercise policy for Section 16 reporting persons in which the Section 16 reporting person obtains any credit extension from the broker or other third party of his or her choice and (not the issuer) and results in the issuer being paid the exercise price on the day of exercise.

- Obtain powers of attorney with multiple attorneys-in-fact from all Section 16 reporting persons.

- Apply for EDGAR access codes for all Section 16 reporting persons. Section 16 reporting persons can obtain a Form ID for obtaining EDGAR access codes from the SEC at *http://www.sec.gov/about/forms/formid.pdf*.

Forfeiture of compensation and stock sale profits by CEOs and CFOs upon restatements due to misconduct

Section 304 of the 2002 Act requires forfeiture of certain bonuses and profits realized by the CEO and CFO of a company that is required to prepare an accounting restatement due to the company's "material noncompliance, as a result of misconduct, with any financial reporting requirement under the securities laws." Specifically, the CEO and CFO must reimburse to the company any bonus or other incentive- or equity-based compensation received, and any profit realized from the sale of the company's stock sold, during a specified recapture period. Reimbursement is required whether or not the CEO or CFO engaged in or knew of the misconduct. The "recapture period" is the 12-month period following "the first public issuance or filing with the SEC (whichever first occurs) of the financial document embodying such financial reporting requirement."

It is unclear how one determines when targeted compensation is "received" for purposes of Section 304. The application of Section 304 of the 2002 Act to common executive compensation arrangements will be difficult to apply in practice. For example, is equity-based compensation "received" upon the grant or exercise of a stock option, or both? Is restricted stock "received" upon grant or vesting? Are performance-based nonqualified deferred compensation benefits "received" in the year earned or in the year of actual receipt? Do constructive principles similar to those under the tax laws apply? These and other types of interpretative questions will require regulatory guidance or legislative clarification.

This provision applies to both U.S. and non-U.S. companies. The SEC may exercise its authority to exempt non-U.S. companies.

Freeze on extraordinary payments to directors and officers

Section 1103 of the 2002 Act allows the SEC, during an investigation of an issuer or its directors, officers, partners, controlling persons, or other employees, to seek a temporary order in federal court requiring the issuer to escrow "extraordinary payments" to such person for 45 to 90 days (or, if such person is charged with a violation of the securities laws, until conclusion of the proceedings). There is no definition of "extraordinary payments" other than to indicate that it includes compensation. "Extraordinary payments" might include bonuses, stock option exercises, payments under a nonqualified deferred compensation plan, and severance pay.

This provision applies to both U.S. and non-U.S. companies. The SEC may exercise its authority to exempt non-U.S. companies.

2. SEC Rulings and No-Action Letters

Between 2001 and 2005, the SEC issued many rulings on equity-related accounting, corporate governance, and plan operations. We highlight key rulings below. However, because of significant changes to the law during that period, many of these rulings (particularly those dealing with accounting issues before FAS123(R)) are reviewed here for their historical value only. Readers should be careful to note the date of any ruling before relying upon it.

In 2002, the SEC ruled that companies could not continue to exclude "broad-based" equity compensation plans (loosely interpreted to mean most employees were eligible for awards, even if they never got them) from shareholder approval; since the 2002 ruling went into effect, shareholders have had the right to vote on new plans and material modifications of existing plans in many more circumstances than before. Then, in 2003, the SEC approved a major rewrite of shareholder approval rules issued by the NYSE and the NASDAQ. Among other things, the rules require that brokers obtain instructions from shareholders on stock held in street name and require shareholder approval of repricings and material modifications of plans. Qualified plans, employment inducement awards, qualified plans under ERISA, and parallel excess plans can be excluded.

Over the years, plan operation rulings have allowed companies to use unregistered stock in a bonus plan, allowed automatic enrollment in an ESPP for a pre-IPO company, and created a simplified procedure for closely held companies to create an internal stock market. Increasing shareholder activism prompted more proxy fights over requiring companies to base option awards on performance or that companies expense options. Most (but not all) of the rulings to date require that proposals on these matters be included.

In a major proposal that will be fleshed out in 2006, the SEC required substantially greater disclosure of executive compensation, including equity awards. Companies must now disclose the number of securities to be issued if outstanding options, warrants, and other rights are exercised and the weighted average exercise price of the shares to be issued, as well as the number of securities available for further issuance other than any included above.

Accounting issues

SEC says option exercise rescissions require variable accounting

In *Exemptive Order, Securities and Exchange Act of 1934: "Repricing"* (Mar. 21, 2001), the SEC issued guidance stating that if a company allows employees with options to turn in shares obtained through the exercise of stock options in exchange for new options, then this will trigger variable accounting procedures. For the rescission to be effective, the shares must be turned in during the same tax year the employee exercised the option.

The policy of allowing "rescissions" on options was controversial. It is easiest to understand how a rescission works through an example. Assume Bill got an option at $20 per share in 1995. In January 2000, he exercised the option. The share price was now $45. It does not matter whether the option is an ISO or a nonqualified option. An incentive option will become a nonqualified option if the employee turns in the shares because they will not have been held long enough to qualify as an ISO. By December, the share price had tumbled to $15. The company allowed Bill to turn in the shares and get new options with the same price and terms as the old ones. The price Bill paid to exercise the options was returned to him, and Bill returned any dividends paid during the period he held the shares. From an income tax standpoint, the argument is that nothing has happened—the old options have been canceled, the employee has no tax due, and the company does not get a tax deduction.

The SEC, relying on the accounting standard then in effect (APB 25), issued guidance on rescissions saying that the practice creates a variable accounting requirement, meaning that, unlike with conventional stock option practices, the cost of option must be reflected on the company financial statements. The SEC allowed a transition period, however, saying that the treatment applied only to rescissions granted after January 1, 2001.

For rescissions before 2001, the company had to record a charge to earnings equal to any tax deduction it lost as a result of the rescission (the $25 spread between the $20 exercise price and the $45 share price, in our example), plus any additional cost represented by the excess of the share price over the option price at the time of the rescission ($5 in this example

For rescissions after January 1, 2001, the company had to use "marked-to-market" variable accounting, meaning it recorded an expense each quarter representing the current difference between the option price ($20) and the market price of the shares, a process that can result in a substantial accounting charge. This would go on until the options were no longer in effect, either because they had been exercised, they had lapsed, or they were forfeited. In addition, the company had to disclose the terms of the rescission in its financial statements. In its stockholder equity section, the company had to show the initial exercise and subsequent rescission. Rescinded shares had to be included in the calculation of "basic" earnings per share while the shares were outstanding, and any cash flow results needed to be discussed in management's "discussion and analysis."

Plan operations

Oracle can use unregistered stock in bonus plan

In *Oracle Corp.* (SEC No-Action Letter, June 13, 2000), the Securities and Exchange Commission allowed Oracle to use unregistered stock for a stock bonus plan because the employees were given the stock as a bonus, they were not asked to buy it, and the percentage of total shares involved was very small.

Automatic enrollment process does not require securities registration

In *American Bar Association* (SEC No-Action Letter, July 25, 2000), the SEC considered a closely held company that had created an automatic enrollment option for a Section 423 ESPP. Employees could make payroll deductions into the plan before the company's initial public offering, but they could not purchase shares until after it. The SEC ruled that simply setting up the enrollment procedure and taking the deductions is not an offer to sell securities because the employee would not make that choice until the end of the option purchase period, at which time the company would be public.

SEC issues no-action letter in Martha Stewart Omnimedia options-for-bonus exchange program

In *Martha Stewart Omnimedia, Inc.*, SEC No-Action Letter (Nov. 7, 2003), the SEC staff, without commenting on the merits of the submission, allowed Martha Stewart Omnimedia (MSO) to proceed with an offer to allow employees to exchange their underwater options for a cash bonus.

The company sought the no-action letter to confirm that the SEC would not take enforcement action against the offer under Rules 13e-4(f)(5) and 14e-1(c) under the Securities Act of 1934, which requires tender offers companies make for their own shares not to be fraudulent actions or to unfairly favor one group of interests over another. Similar no-action letters have been sought and granted in other option exchange programs, including Microsoft's well-publicized 2003 program.

In this case, MSO offered a cash bonus to about three-quarters of its employees who held underwater options. MSO stock fell sharply in the prior two years, partly because of adverse publicity concerning its founder. Employees below the vice president level could exchange their underwater options during 2003 for a cash bonus to be paid in June 2004. Employees had to remain with the company until then to receive the payment. One issue of concern was whether this delay in payment violated the sections of the rules dealing with "prompt payment" to shareholders. MSO counsel argued that this delay in payment was similar to other option exchange programs, many of which require a six-month delay. The delay also served to encourage employees to stay with the company, and, counsel argued, should be seen as part of an appropriate compensation policy. Because the offering was structured so that employees knew specifically what the terms and conditions were, counsel argued that the tender offer was also not fraudulent or misleading. The staff of the SEC agreed to issue a no-action letter but did not comment on the merits of the case.

Comcast option liquidity program cleared by SEC staff

In 2004, Comcast became the first company to adopt the model created by Microsoft and J.P. Morgan over a year earlier to provide liquidity for underwater stock options. Under the arrangement, employees could tender their options to Comcast. J.P. Morgan purchased the options from Comcast at an arm's-length value (computed over an averaging period), and Comcast paid the J.P. Morgan price over to employees. The SEC staff, pursuant to Rule 13-e-4(f)(2)(ii), allowed Comcast to terminate the withdrawal rights to tendered options at the end of the employee's election period and, under Rule 13-e(f)(8)(i), permitted Comcast to exclude some options and optionees from the program. The staff said it would not object to the pricing structure. *No Action, Interpretive and/or Exemptive Letter: Comcast Corporation* (Oct. 7, 2004).

The approach allowed Comcast employees with underwater options to get some (albeit usually small) value for them. Comcast, meanwhile, benefitted from having fewer options outstanding, options that really have little incentive or compensation benefit. That gave Comcast more flexibility in creating a more effective equity program. J.P. Morgan, of course, hoped that it will be able to buy the options at a price that will make them profitable in the long run. To read the full letter, see *http://sec.gov/divisions/copfin/cfnoaction/comcast100704.htm*.

SEC issues no-action letter for internal stock market

In a no-action letter dated October 20, 2005, to James Dvorak of Venable LLP, the SEC staff stated that an internal stock market operated by a closely held company did not have to register as a broker-dealer. The company, TEOCO, is a small fast-growing, technology company in Fairfax, VA. It is employee-owned (the name is an acronym for "The Employee Owned Company") by 64 shareholders, all of whom are current or former employees or directors, plus 130 current and former employees and directors who hold options. Its plan provides for periodic trades at an appraised value, with the company acting as the go-between. The plan will operate within Rule 701 under the Securities Act of 1933 (a rule that, among other things, exempts from registration requirements sales of shares equal to less than 15% of a company's total shares in any one year that are offered as part of an employee compensation plan), and no sales to or purchases by individuals otherwise disqualified from purchasing or selling shares will be allowed.

TEOCO will arrange for periodic trades, most likely once or twice a year. A plan committee will oversee the process. Dates will be set in advance, detailed information mailed to employees, and an informational meeting held. Employees can offer to sell shares they own or buy additional shares. The company established minimums and maximums on the number of shares that must be purchased or can be sold. As submitted, the plan limits shares offered for sale to not more than 50% of what an individual owns.

The company acts as the sole buyer and seller, rather than having transactions occurring between individuals. An independent third-party appraiser sets the sale price in advance, but the price must be revisited if there are material changes in the interim. Employees indicate how many shares they want to sell or buy and submit this to the company.

In the unlikely event the number of sale and purchase offers is equal, the company buys all the shares for sale and resells them all. More likely, there will be an imbalance. If there are more purchase offers, the company buys all the shares for sale, then parcels out remaining shares based on an equitable formula designed to give preference to smaller holders. If there are more sellers, the company accepts all offers to buy and then allocates the remaining number according to the same formula.

Because the company is buying and selling for its own account, not acting as an agent (especially a commissioned agent) of the sellers or buyers, the SEC accepted the argument that it is not a broker-dealer.

Registration exemptions

Independent sales representatives can get options under Rule 701 exemption

In *Wright Acquisition Holdings, Inc.* (SEC No-Action Letter), a company wanted sales representatives to be able to get stock options under a Rule 701 exemption from securities offerings registration requirements. The SEC allowed the offering, provided that the sales representatives warranted that they received most of their income from the company, agreed to non-compete, non-disclosure and non-solicitation agreements, and that marketing the company's products or services was the sales representatives' major line of business.

Arizona denies request for automatic exemption from securities registration for stock option plan

The Arizona Securities Division denied a request for a no-action letter from World Internet Holdings, Inc., on its stock option plan. The company was seeking an exemption for the plan from securities registration requirements. The company said its plan would meet the requirements of Rule 701 for exemption under the Securities Act of 1933. The state gave no reason for its denial. The action does underline the fact that just because a plan qualifies for an exemption under federal law, it does not necessarily qualify under state law.

Google, SEC settle over pre-IPO options

In *In re Google Inc.*, SEC Admin. Proc. File No. 3-11795 (Jan. 13, 2005), Google settled SEC and state charges concerning its alleged failure to register options issued before its initial public offering (IPO) in 2004. At issue was $80 million in options Google issued in the two years before the IPO. The SEC said Google failed to register the securities, as required by federal and state law absent a specific exemption (such as Rule 701), and to provide financial disclosure, as required by both federal and state (California) law.

Google had stated it believed it could rely on an exemption from the requirements. Under federal law, offers to a company's employees, directors, general partners, trustees, officers, or certain consultants (those providing services to a company similar to what an employer might hire someone to do, but not consultants who help raise capital) can be made under a written compensation agreement. For total sales not exceeding $5 million during a 12-month period to the specified class of people above, companies must comply with anti-fraud disclosure rules; for sales of more than this amount, companies must disclose additional information, including risk factors, copies of the plans under which the offerings are made, and certain financial statements. These disclosures must be made to all shareholders. Optionees are included under this requirement. Google could have been exempted under this exemption, but the SEC found that it did not comply with the rules. In addition, securities laws also require public disclosure of relevant financial issues and risks for any issuance of options of more than $5 million in a year. Google did not make such disclosures, fearing that the information would put the company at a competitive disadvantage. Google had previously addressed the situation by offering employees the right to have their options repurchased at varying prices, all of which were far below what Google's stock eventually opened at in its IPO. There were few takers.

Reporting and disclosure issues

SEC issues equity compensation plan disclosure rules

In Release No. 33-8048 (Dec. 21, 2001), the SEC set out the final rules for disclosure of equity compensation plan information, adopting amendments under the Exchange Act that enhance disclosure requirements applicable to annual reports on Form 10-K and Form 10-KSB (annual reports) and to proxy and information statements filed in connection with annual meetings (annual meeting materials). Generally, the final rule prescribes a new form of stock plan disclosure table that must be filed each year with annual reports and with annual meeting materials in any year when any compensation plan is submitted for shareholder action. The table breaks down equity plans into two categories: those that have been approved by shareholders, and those that have not been approved (including individual arrangements and plans assumed in an M&A transaction). For each category, the company must supply the following data in tabulated form:

1. Column A: Number of securities to be issued upon exercise of outstanding options, warrants, and rights;
2. Column B: Weighted-average exercise price of outstanding options, warrants, and rights; and
3. Column C: Number of securities remaining available for future issuance under equity compensation plans (excluding securities reflected in column A).

The data may be aggregated within each category. For each non-approved plan or individual arrangement, the company must file copies of the documents (unless immaterial) and provide a brief narrative describing the material features of the plan or arrangement. This requirement for a narrative description may be satisfied by cross-referencing information already set out in the company's financial statements in accordance with FAS 123(R). The final rule became effective on March 15, 2002, for annual reports filed with respect to fiscal years ending on and after that date, and on June 15, 2002, for annual meeting materials filed on or after that date.

Shareholder rights

SEC requires companies to allow shareholder proposals on stock plans

Changing its position from that stated in previous rulings (see below), the Securities and Exchange Commission (SEC) ruled in Division of Corporation Finance Staff Legal Bulletin No. 14A (July 12, 2002) that companies cannot exclude shareholder proposals under the Rule 14a-8 exclusion that allows companies to avoid shareholder votes on proposals dealing with "ordinary business matters," such as employee compensation. Some companies had been relying on this rule to preclude shareholder votes on equity plans that were broad-based. A prior SEC ruling had allowed this interpretation, but the new ruling reverses this stand in cases where the plan would result in "material dilution." NASDAQ and the NYSE had made similar proposals, but the SEC ruling will apply to all public companies, wherever they are traded. The change was based on the SEC's conclusion that the social and economic environment had changed, making equity compensation an issue beyond ordinary business. For more details, go to *http://www.sec.gov/interps/legal/cfslb14a.htm*.

Specifically, the SEC ruled on certain scenarios. The following material is taken verbatim from the ruling:

- *Proposals that focus on equity compensation plans that may be used to compensate only senior executive officers and directors.* As has been our position since 1992, companies may not rely on rule 14a-8(i)(7) to omit these proposals from their proxy materials.

- *Proposals that focus on equity compensation plans that may be used to compensate senior executive officers, directors and the general workforce.* If the proposal seeks to obtain shareholder approval of all such equity compensation plans, without regard to their potential dilutive effect, a company may rely on rule 14a-8(i)(7) to omit the proposal from its proxy materials. If the proposal seeks to obtain shareholder approval of all such equity compensation plans that potentially would result in material dilution to existing shareholders, a company may not rely on rule 14a-8(i)(7) to omit the proposal from its proxy materials.

- *Proposals that focus on equity compensation plans that may be used to compensate the general workforce only, with no senior executive officer or director participation.* If the proposal seeks to obtain shareholder approval of all such equity compensation plans, without regard to their potential dilutive effect, a company may rely on rule 14a-8(i)(7) to omit the proposal from its proxy materials. If the proposal seeks to obtain shareholder approval of all such equity compensation plans that potentially would result in material dilution to existing shareholders, a company may not rely on rule 14a-8(i)(7) to omit the proposal from its proxy materials.

SEC changes rule on voting on stock option expensing

In a December 6, 2002, letter to the United Brotherhood of Carpenters and Joiners, Martin Dunn, the SEC's deputy director of corporation finance, said that following an SEC review of the matter, "in the future, we will not treat shareholder proposals requesting the expensing of stock options as relating to ordinary business matters." The SEC had already been going in this direction in two prior letters on this matter, but this new letter made it clear that this will be SEC policy generally, not just on a case-by-case basis. Prior to these letters, companies could exclude proxies asking for expensing saying that they related to ordinary business issues not within the scope of proxy requirements. The ruling reverses the rulings below (*Meredith Corp.* and *Sysco Corp.*).

SEC rules companies can exclude shareholder proposals on option expensing

In separate rulings, the staff of the Securities and Exchange Commission's Division of Corporation Finance advised companies that they were not required to allow shareholder proposals on expensing options. In the first (*Meredith Corp.*, SEC No-Action Letter, Aug. 9, 2002), the staff ruled that the decision of the Meredith Corporation to not allow a shareholder proposal to require the company to expense options was an "ordinary business matter" and therefore not subject to a required shareholder vote. In the second (*Sysco Corp.*, SEC No-Action Letter, Aug. 30, 2002), the staff said that under Rule 14a-8(I)(6), a proposal to require that the company account for executive options only was excludable because such an accounting procedure was not consistent with FAS 123. Under that rule, if a company chooses to expense some options, it has to expense all of them. The company therefore lacked the authority to implement the proposal. The staff also said that, as in *Meredith*, expensing was an "ordinary business matter" and thus proposals on it could be excluded. However, see above for subsequent SEC rulings that indicate a new direction the SEC will take on these issues.

Performance-based options not excludable from shareholder votes

In letters to Goldman Sachs, Texas Instruments, and Fluor Corporation, the staff of the SEC Division of Corporate Finance ruled that companies cannot exclude shareholder proposals to require that options be performance-based as "ordinary business matters." The letters follow a trend from the SEC to require companies to allow votes on how option plans are structured and accounted for. For details, see *Goldman Sachs Group Inc.*, SEC No-Action Letter (Jan. 3, 2003), *Texas Instruments Inc.*, SEC No-Action Letter (Jan. 8, 2003), and *Fluor Corp.*, SEC No-Action Letter (Mar. 10, 2003).

The first two letters, *Goldman Sachs* and *Texas Instruments,* addressed identically worded proposals asking the respective corporate boards to:

> adopt an executive compensation policy that all future stock option grants to senior executives shall be performance-based. For the purpose of this resolution, a stock option is performance-based if the option exercise price is indexed or linked to an industry peer group stock performance index so that the options have value only to the extent that the Company's stock price performance exceeds the peer group performance.

Goldman Sachs argued that it could not accept the Massachusetts Carpenters Pension & Annuity Funds' proposal because the company was submitting its own proposal on equity compensation, one that provided a compensation committee with discretion about how to issue equity grants, including options, restricted stock, stock rights, and other awards. The proposal did not have any requirements for guidelines about how these awards would be issued. Under Securities Exchange Act Rule 14a-8(i)(9), companies can exclude shareholder proposals from a proxy statement if they conflict with a company proposal to be presented at the same meeting. Goldman argued that if both proposals were accepted, the compensation committee would be given total discretion under one accepted proposal and limited discretion under the other. The SEC staff disagreed, saying that it did not find the company's interpretation of Rule 14a-8(i)(9) compelling.

In the Texas Instruments case, the company said it intended to submit a long-term compensation plan for shareholder approval in 2003. A board committee would have discretion to decide what kinds of equity awards would go to whom, within certain broad parameters. The company argued that the discretionary proposal would conflict with the Central Laborers' Pension Fund's more restrictive proposal and should therefore be excluded. The SEC staff again disagreed, although it did say that some of the supporting statements for the Carpenters' proposal were misleading and said they would have to be revised for the proposal to be acceptable.

The Fluor case involved a proposal by the International Brotherhood of Electrical Workers' Pension Benefit Fund to require that options for key employees be indexed to an industry peer group. As in the other two cases, the company argued that it could exclude the proposal under Section 14a-8(i)(9) on the grounds that it directly conflicted with a proposal Fluor itself was making at the 2003 meeting. The company also said that the proposal was "micro-managing" and thus could be excluded under Rule 14(a)-8(i)(7) as dealing with the ordinary business of the company, and that it also fell under Rule 14a-8(i)(3) because it contained false and misleading statements. The SEC staff disagreed, although as with Texas Instruments, it did say that some of the supporting statements for the IBEW proposal could be false or misleading and would have to be amended or dropped if they were to be included in the proxy materials.

Executive pay proposal can be omitted from proxy as too vague

However, the SEC has not approved all executive pay proposals from shareholders. In *Woodward Governor Co.*, SEC No-Action Letter (Nov. 26, 2003), the staff said the company could exclude a proposal on executive pay as being too vague. Shareholder Gerald English had proposed that "the board of Woodward Governor Company implement a policy for compensation for the executives in upper management (that being plant managers to board members), based on stock growth. This would focus the management team on the goal of increasing stock value." The SEC staff said this could be omitted on several grounds, including Rule 14a-8(i)(3) under the 1934 Securities Exchange Act, because it is vague and "inherently misleading." The language covers all of executive compensation, so it could result in executives getting no pay in a bad year. Based on a supporting statement from English describing a formula for calculating pay, in a good year, executives might only receive $10,000, but the proposal was not clear enough to know just how it would work.

SEC rules performance-based options may not be excluded from shareholder ballot

In *Crescent Real Estate Equities Co.*, SEC No-Action Letter (Apr. 5, 2004), the SEC ruled that a shareholder proposal that a significant portion of future stock option grants to senior executives be performance-based could not be excluded from a shareholder ballot. The company argued the proposal was too vague and contained misleading statements. The SEC said the statement did need to be amended to correct the errors but that the proposal could go forward.

The proposal was submitted by the Board of Trustees of the International Brotherhood of Electrical Workers Pension Benefit Fund. The proposal urged that a significant portion of future options be indexed options, premium-priced options, or performance-vested options. Counsel for the company argued that the proposal could be excluded under the 1934 Securities Exchange Act Rule 14a-8(j)(i)(3) because it was too vague. It did not name which specific officers would be covered, what "significant" meant, or whether the grant of such options should affect cash compensation. Counsel argued the company already based executive compensation on performance.

The SEC staff agreed that some of the proposal had inaccuracies and some was too vague but said that if it were amended to correct this, it could go forward.

SEC counsel's office allows option proposal to be excluded

Shareholder Gerald English submitted a proposal to Woodward Governor Corporation to eliminate all stock option programs. Relying on Rule 14a-8(i)(7), on September 29, 2004, SEC Special Counsel Heather Maples signed a staff decision that the proposal could be excluded because the option program did not just cover senior executives and directors but also extended to "key management worker members as potential recipients." The company had provided options to 20 employees who were not officers or directors.

SEC approves shareholder approval rules for equity compensation plans

Effective June 30, 2003, companies listed on the New York Stock Exchange and the NASDAQ must obtain shareholder approval for all equity compensation plans, with certain very narrow exceptions.

For the NYSE, the new rules are Section 303A(8) of the Listed Company Manual. For the NASDAQ, the new rules are NASD Rules 4310(c)(17)(a) and 4320(e)(15)(A). The rules are very similar to each other. The most significant exception is that the NYSE rules prohibit broker voting on these issues; NADSAQ already does not allow broker voting on any issue. In effect, therefore, the two sets of rules are the same for broker voting as to shareholder approval of equity plans. Other inconsistencies are minor; probably the most significant is that the NYSE rules require the company to submit in writing to the SEC reasons why it is relying on one of the material modification exemptions; the NASDAQ is considering adding such a rule. A summary of the rules is as follows. Details can be found at *http://www.sec.gov/rules/sro/34-48108.htm.*

1. *Scope:* All equity compensation plans, and any material revisions to these plans, must be approved by shareholders, with certain narrow exceptions, as outlined below.

2. *Equity compensation plans defined:* An equity compensation plan includes any plan or other arrangement to deliver securities to employees, including options. The term does not include dividend reinvestment plans or plans that allow employees, directors, or other service providers to buy shares on the open market for current fair market value.

3. *Material modification:* "Material" is not defined by these rules, although it specially does not include the limitation of rights and benefits associated with a plan; only modifications expanding employee rights and benefits are covered. The list of covered modifications includes:

    a. A material increase in the number of shares available, other than for stock splits, corporate reorganizations, and similar arrangements. Evergreen plans require approval for each increase unless the plan has a term of not more than 10 years. If the increase is not pursuant to a formula, then shareholders must approve each increase. A requirement that grants be made out of treasury or repurchased shares will not, in itself, be considered a formula.

    b. An expansion of the types of awards available under the plan or of the class of employees, directors, or other service providers eligible to participate.

    c. A material extension of the term of the plan.

d. A material change in the method of determining the strike price of options, such as changing the fair market value from the closing date on grant to the average of the high and low price on the date of grant.

   e. The deletion or limitation of any provision prohibiting repricing.

4. *Repricings:* Unless a plan specifically permits repricing, it is considered to prohibit it. Any actual repricing other than an exchange offer that started before the effective date of these rules is thus considered a material modification. Canceling an option and substituting a new award pursuant to a merger, acquisition, spin-off, or similar transaction is not included.

5. *Employment inducement awards:* If the company's independent compensation committee approves them, inducement awards to new hires may be made without shareholder approval. Companies must disclose in a press release, and in written material for the NYSE, a description of the award, its terms, the number of shares and its recipient. "New hires" includes rehires of previous employees following a "bona fide" period of non-employment.

6. *Mergers and acquisitions:* Shareholder approval is not required to replace options or other awards in a transaction. Shares available for award at a closely held company that is acquired may be used in post-acquisition grants, provided that the plan existed before the merger or acquisition being contemplated. The time the shares are available cannot be extended after the transaction.

7. *Qualified plans:* Employee stock ownership plans, other Section 401 plans invested in company stock (401(k), profit sharing, and stock bonus plans), and Section 423 ESPPs do not require approval.

8. *Parallel excess plans:* These are plans that provide additional company contributions or employee deferrals into qualified plans that limit the total amount of compensation that can be considered or place ceilings on the total amounts that can be contributed. Companies sometimes make up the difference that would be allowed if these ceilings did not exist; the contributions or deferrals are not tax-favored. Investments in equity in these plans would be exempted from shareholder

approval requirements. The plan must cover all or substantially all affected employees, its terms must be the same for those covered, it must parallel the terms for the qualified plans, and no one can receive compensation in excess of 25% of cash compensation. Plans meetings these rules will not require approval.

9. *Transition rules:* Plans adopted before the SEC's approval of these rules are not subject to shareholder approval requirements unless and until they are materially revised. Discretionary plans can issue additional awards only for a limited time, specifically (1) the next annual meeting at which directors are elected that occurs 180 days after the effective date of these rules; (2) the first anniversary of these rules; or (3) the expiration of the plan, whichever comes first. Similarly, formula plans that have not been previously approved by shareholders and do not have a term of 10 years or less can make additional grants after these rules become effective, but only within the transition period limits. Formula plans that are approved after the rules are effective can continue to be used longer than the transition period if amended to provide for a term of 10 years or less, or if the grants are made only from shares immediately available after the effective date.

10. *Broker voting:* In what may be the most significant hurdle of the new rules, broker-held shares ("street name" shares) cannot be voted by proxy by the brokers unless the beneficial owner provides specific instructions. This new rule is effective 90 days after the effective date of the rules.

Stock exchange rulings

NYSE fines Citigroup for violations in its supervision of WorldCom options program

On October 29, 2003, the New York Stock Exchange fined Citigroup $1 million for failing to properly oversee a group of its registered representatives in Atlanta who handled stock option exercises for WorldCom employees between 1998 and 2001. The exchange also disciplined the firm's Atlanta branch manager for the same issue. Both agreed to the exchange's punishments without admitting or denying misconduct.

The issue revolved around a well-publicized pattern in the Atlanta office of advising some WorldCom employees to exercise their options with margin loans, then hold on to the shares in anticipation of further gains and possible tax benefits. When the stock declined, the employees, many of whose assets were substantially concentrated in WorldCom stock, faced margin calls, often forcing them to sell other assets on demand. The NYSE found that the representatives did not have the "extensive training" the firm claimed they had, or even specific training in the options area. The exchange concluded that the margin loans were imprudent in light of the risks involved.

The action against Citigroup is the first in what may be a series of actions against other brokers in the Atlanta area.

Microsoft employee wins case against UBS

On January 27, 2005, a Microsoft employee won a judgment from a National Association of Securities Dealers (NASD) arbitration panel against UBS for urging him to exercise his stock options with a margin loan (NASD Case No. 03-00703, unpublished). UBS and a number of brokerage firms (against whom actions are still pending) actively promoted a strategy in which employees would use margin loans to exercise their ISOs. The employees would then try to hold on to the stock for at least one year to benefit from lower ISO tax treatment. Unfortunately, in the post-market-boom crash, their stock often fell quickly, especially in technology companies. When the stock price fell below the margin call requirement, employees had to sell, triggering ordinary income tax if the stock had not been held for at least one year from exercise and two years from the grant of the option. The employees were left in a net loss position. Not only had they sold their stock at what often was a price lower than they bought it for, but they also had to pay taxes on the difference between the exercise price and price at purchase, often a very large amount.

Employees alleged both that the margin loan approach induced them to take excessive risk and that the brokerages should have used a risk management strategy, such as a stop-loss sale price that would have covered the taxes and the loan or a hedging strategy using put and call options to create a "zero-cost collar." The employee in this case received $237,338, the amount such a hedging strategy would have saved.

Part III:
Table of Cases

Table of Cases

A

Adamany v. Superior Court of Los Angeles County, 2002 Cal. App. Unpub. LEXIS 6823 (July 25, 2002), 46

Adams v. Louisiana-Pacific Corp., 284 F. Supp. 2d 311 (W.D. N.C. 2003), 24

AirTouch Communications Inc. v. Nott-Kilfoil, 2002 Cal. App. Unpub. LEXIS 11621 (Cal. Ct. App. Dec. 16, 2002) (unpublished), 34

Alexander v. Codemasters Group Ltd., 104 Cal. App. 4th 129 (2002), 16

Allen v. Levey (In re Allen) (226 B.R. 857, Bankr. N.D. Ill 1998), 46

Applewhite v. Computer Associates International, 3-01CV0853-R (N.D. Tex. Apr. 18, 2002), 6

Ayyad v. Rashid, 2003 Wash. App. LEXIS 383 (Wash. Ct. App. Mar. 10, 2003), 60

B

Baccanti v. Morton, 434 Mass. 787 (2001), 53

Bailey v. Grey, Siefert & Co., Inc., 752 N.Y.S. 2d 646 (N.Y. App. Div.-1st Dec. 31, 2002), 6

Bau v. Actamed Corporation, 562 S.E. 2d 734 (Ga. Ct. App. 2002), cert. denied, 123 S. Ct. 1487 (2003), 35

Bedrosian v. Tenet Healthcare Corp., B166742 (Cal. Ct. App. Oct. 28, 2003), modified November 25, 2003, cert. denied S121071 (Cal. Feb. 18, 2004) (unpublished), 31

Black v. Hoffman, No. 00-1797 (4th Cir. Apr. 13, 2001) (unpublished), 15

Bohan v. Honeywell International Inc., 366 F.3d 606 (8th Cir. 2004), 34

Bors v. Duberstein, No. 03 C 4636 (N.D. Ill. July 1, 2004), 16

Braun v. CMGI, 64 Fed. App'x. 301 (2d Cir. 2003) (unpublished), 15

Brebaugh v. Deane, 211 Ariz. 95 (Ariz. Ct. App.-Div. 1 2005), 49

Brown v. Coleman Company, Inc. 220 F.3d 1180 (10th Cir. 2000), 46

Brown v. Nortel Networks, 2002 Mass. Super. LEXIS 159 (2002), 24

Butvin v. Doubleclick, Inc., 2001 WL 22812 (S.D.N.Y. Mar. 7, 2001) (unpublished), 14

C

Chumbley v. Beckmann, 110 Wash. App. 871, 43 P.3d 53 (Wash. Ct. App. 2002), reversed and remanded, No. 72539-0 (Wash. Aug. 14, 2003), 59

Clance v. Clance, 127 S.W.3d 716 (Mo. Ct. App. 2004), 54

Cochran v. Quest Software, 328 F.3d 1 (1st Cir. 2003), 7

Crampton v. Abbott Laboratories, 186 F. Supp. 2nd 850 (N.D. Ill. 2002), 8

D

D'Oliveira v. Rare Hospitality Int'l Inc., 2003 R.I. Super. LEXIS 28 (Feb. 13, 2003), 6

Dell Computer Corp. v. Rodriguez, 2004 U.S. App. LEXIS 23393 (5th Cir. Nov. 8, 2004), 27

DiLorenzo v. Valve & Primer Corp., 779 N.E.2d 280 (Ill. App. Ct. Sept. 6, 2002), vacated and remanded 785 N.E.2d 860 (Ill. Apr. 2, 2003), remanded 2003 Ill. App. LEXIS 710 (Ill. App. Ct. June 6, 2003), 16

Donaldson v. Digital General Systems, 168 S.W.3d 909 (Tex. App.-5th July 22, 2005), 5, 10

Dubbs v. Net Value Holdings, 2003 Cal. App. Unpub. LEXIS 999 (Jan. 30, 2003) (unpublished), 34

E

Edwards v. Schrader-Bridgeport International, Inc., 205 F. Supp. 2d 3 (N.D.N.Y. 2002), 30

Elgaway v. Watkins-Johnson Company (HO22472, Cal. Ct. App. 6th Dist. June 5, 2002), 35

Emmenegger v. Bull Moose Tube Co., 324 F.3d 616 (8th Cir. 2003), 43

F

Falkowski v. Imation Corp., 132 Cal. App. 4th 499 (Cal. App. 2005), 37

Falkowski v. Imation Corp., 132 Cal. App. 4th 499 (Cal. Ct. App. 2005), 42

Falkowski v. Imation Corp., 309 F.3d 1123 (9th Cir. 2002), amended 320 F.3d 905 (9th Cir. 2003), 42

First Marblehead Corp. v. House, 401 F. Supp. 2d 152 (D. Mass. 2005), 10

Fisher v. Fisher, 564 Pa. 586 (Pa. 2001), 57

Fix v. Quantum Industrial Partners LDC, 374 F.3d 549 (7th Cir. 2004), 35

Fountain v. Fountain, No. 01-14 (N.C. Ct. App. Feb. 5, 2002), 56

Fox v. Fox, 2002 Ohio 2010 (Ohio Ct. App. April 25, 2002), 57

G

Galdieri v. Monsanto Co., 245 F. Supp. 2d 636 (E.D. Pa. 2002), 23

Gelhaus v. Fingerhut Companies, Inc. (Minn. Ct. App. May 7, 2002) (unpublished), 12

Grimes v. Alteon, Inc., 804 A. 2d 256 (Del. July 19, 2002), 16

H

Hanig v. Qualcomm, Inc., No. D038513 (Cal. Ct. App. Dec. 6, 2002) (unpublished), 29

Harrison v. NetCentric Corp.,433 Mass. 465 (2001), 20

Heitt v. Heitt, No. 03-812 (Ark. Ct. App. Apr. 14, 2004), 50

Heller-Loren v. Appuzio, No. A-0494-2T3 (N.J. App. Div. Aug. 3, 2004), 56

Hilen v. Commissioner, T.C.M. 2005-226 (2005), 63

Hmelyar v. Phoenix Controls, 2003 WL 21436530 (Ill. Ct. App. June 17, 2003), 23

Hopfer v. Hopfer, 757 A. 2nd 673 (Conn. App. Ct. 2000), 52

Hopmayer v. Aladdin Indus., LLC, No. M2003-01583-COA-R3-DV (Tenn. Ct. App. June 9, 2004), 16

Hurd v. Spine-Tech, Inc., 2002 Minn. App. LEXIS 1249 (Minn. Ct. App. Nov. 12, 2002), 35

I

IBM v. Bajorek, 191 F.3d 1033 (9th Cir. 1999), 27
Ingram v. Rencor Controls, Inc., No. 02-58-P-C (D. Me. Apr. 11, 2003), 7
Ingram v. Rencor Controls Inc., No. 02-58-P-C (D. Me. Apr. 11, 2003), 15
In re Clapes, N. 818992 (N.Y. Div. of Tax Appeals Sept. 18, 2003), 68
In re Cower (No. 294394, Sept. 20, 2005), 65
In re Denadai, 259 B.R. 801 (2001), aff'd, Denadai v Preferred Capital Markets Inc. (D. Mass, No. 01-40073-WGY, Nov. 13, 2001), 45
In re Deviny, 2002 Minn. App. LEXIS 1297 (Minn. Ct. App. 2002), 53
In re Marriage of Shui v. Rose, No. 54539-6-I (Wash. Ct. App. Dec. 19, 2005), 58
In re Nehk, 2002 Cal. App. Unpub. LEXIS 1098 (May 14, 2002), 50
In re Pre-Press Graphics Co., 287 B.R. 726 (N.D. Ill. Jan 6, 2003), 44
In re Randall (No. 260104, Mar. 22, 2005), 66
In re the Marriage of Robinson, 201 Ariz. 328 (Ariz. Ct. App. 2002), 49
In re Valence, No. 2000-395 (N.H. May 7, 2002), 55
In re Wick, 276 F.3rd 412 (8th Cir. 2002), 45
Intershop Communications AG v. Superior Court, 104 Cal. App. 4th 191 (Cal. App.-1st 2002), 41

In the Matter of the Petition of E. Randall Stuckless and Jennifer Olson, DTA 819319 (N.Y. Div. of Tax App. July 8, 2004), 67
Irvine v. Capstone Turbine Corp., 2002 Cal. App. Unpub. LEXIS 3603 (Feb. 27, 2002), 21

J

Jensen v. Jensen, 824 So. 2d 315 (Fla. Ct. App. 2002), 52
Jones v. Steinberger (In re Marriage of Steinberger), 91 Cal. App. 4th 1449 (Cal. Ct. App. 2001), review denied (2001), 51

K

Keener v. Convergys Corp., 342 F.3d 1264 (11th Cir. 2003), 26
Kiniry v. Kiniry, No. 21175 (Conn. App. Ct. Aug. 20, 2002), 51
Kushner v. Beverly Enterprises, 317 F.3d 820 (8th Cir. 2002), rehearing en banc denied, 2003 U.S. App. LEXIS 3630 (8th Cir. 2003), 43

L

Levy v. Lucent Techs. Inc., 2003 U.S. Dist. LEXIS 414 (S.D.N.Y. Jan. 14, 2003), 6
Lin v. Qualcomm Inc. (D036196, Cal. Ct. App. Feb. 13, 2002) (unpublished), 15
Lucente v. International Business Machines Corp., 117 F. Supp. 2d 336 (S.D.N.Y. 2000), rev'd and remanded, 310 F.3d 243 (2d Cir. 2002); consent settlement decree entered Oct. 2003, 25
Lynch v. Nortel Networks Corp., 2002 Mass. Super. LEXIS 449 (Mass. Super. Ct. Nov. 4, 2002), 15

M

Mackinley v. Messerchmidt, No. 2137 EDA 2001 (Pa. Super. Ct. Nov. 18, 2002), 57

Martino-Catt v. E.I. Dupont Nemours and Co., 317 F. Supp. 2d 914 (S.D. Iowa Apr. 29, 2004), 16

Medtronic Inc. v. Wohlfeld, 2002 WL 523873 (D. Minn. Mar. 23, 2002), 7

Merlo v. Commissioner, T.C.M. 2005-178 (2005), 64

Miga v. Jensen, 96 S.W.3d 207 (Tex. Oct. 31, 2002), rehearing denied (Feb. 27, 2003), 30

Miller v. PPG Industries, 237 F. Supp. 2d 756 (W.D. Ky. 2002), 44

Miller v. United States, No. C 04-0511 JSW (N.D. Cal. Nov. 22, 2004), 66

Monsanto Co. v. Boustany, 73 S.W.3d 225 (Tex. 2002), 36

Montemayor v. Jacor Communications, Inc., 64 P.3d 916 (Colo. Ct. App. Oct. 24, 2002), cert. denied 2003 Colo. LEXIS 147 (Feb. 24, 2003), 16, 23

Morschbach v. Household Int'l, Inc., 2002 U.S. Dist. LEXIS 1874 (D. Del. Feb. 6, 2002), 37

Moses v. Corning Inc., No. 03-3003 (3rd Cir. July 16, 2004) (unpublished), 6

Moulos v. Lucent Technologies Inc., No. 02 C 550 (N.D. Ill. Nov. 15, 2002), 16

N

No. 84 Employer-Teamster Joint Council Pension Trust Fund v. America West Holding Corp., 320 F.3d 920 (9th Cir. 2003), rehearing en banc denied, 2003 U.S. App., LEXIS 10783 (9th Cir. 2003), cert. denied (2003), 42

Nofs v. Gemini Network, Inc., 2003 Conn. Super. LEXIS 316 (Conn. Super. Ct. Feb. 4, 2003), 21

Noguchi v. Guidant Corp., 2002 Cal. App. Unpub. LEXIS 10210 (Nov. 5, 2002), 6

O

Oatway v. American International Group, Inc., 2002 U.S. Dist. LEXIS 1771 (D. Del. 2002), aff'd, 325 F.3d 184 (3d Cir. 2003), 44

Olander v. Compass Bank, 363 F.3d 560 (5th Cir. 2004), 26

Oracle Corp. v. Falotti, 319 F.3d 1106 (9th Cir. 2003), cert. denied, 540 U.S. 875 (2003), 40

Otley v. Otley, 810 A.2d 1 (Ct. Spec. App. Md. 2002), 53

P

Paolini v. Albertson's Inc., 418 F.3d 1023 (9th Cir. 2005), 23

Paradissiotis v. United States, 49 Fed. Cl. 16 (2001), 41

Pasquel v. AirTouch Communications, Inc., 2002 Cal. App. Unpub. LEXIS 11623 (Cal. Ct. App. Dec. 16, 2002) (unpublished), 34

Pfizer Inc. v. Gilman, 2002 U.S. Dist. LEXIS 2174 (S.D.N.Y. Feb. 13, 2002), 26

Pollen v. Aware, Inc., 53 Mass. App. Ct. 823 (Mass. Ct. App. 2002), 21

R

Raskin v. CyNet, Inc., 131 F. Supp. 2d 906 (S.D. Tex. 2001), 44

Richards v. Jain, 168 F. Supp. 2d 1195 (W.D. Wash. 2001), 15

Robertson v. Robertson, 381 N.J. Super. 199 (N.J. Super. App. Div. 2005), 55

Robinson v. Commissioner, 44 T.C. 20 (1965), 75

Rodriguez v. Vision Corr. Group, Inc., 260 Ga. App. 478 (Mar. 20, 2003), 15

Roller v. Chrysler Corporation, No. 227523 (Mich. Ct. App. Jun. 7, 2002) (unpublished), 12

Romaine v. Colonial Tanning Corp., 301 A.D. 2d 732 (N.Y. App. Div. Jan. 2, 2003), 15

Ruberg v. Ruberg, No. 2D01-2139 (Fla. Dist. Ct. App. Nov. 7, 2003), 52

S

Salsgiver v. America Online, Inc., 147 F. Supp. 2d 1022 (C.D. Col. 2000) aff'd (9th Cir. 2002) (unpublished), 21

Sanchez v. Verio, Inc., No. 01-11341 (5th Cir. Dec. 27, 2004) (unpublished), 11

Schor v. FMS Financial Corp., 814 A2d 1108 (NJ Super. Ct. App. Dec 30, 2002), 37

Scipio v. United National Bankshares, 84 F. Supp. 2d 411 (N.D. W. Va. 2003), 24

Scott v. Workers' Comp. Appeal Bd., 814 A.2d 298 (Pa. Comm. Ct. Jan. 3, 2003), 23

Scribner v. WorldCom, Inc., 249 F.3d 902 (9th Cir. 2001), 11

Scully v. US Watts, Inc., 238 F.3d 497 (3d Cir. 2001), 21, 23, 30

Seraphine v. Aqua Bath Co., 2003 Tenn. App. LEXIS (Tenn. Ct. App. 248 Mar. 28, 2003), 12

Sheils v. Pfizer Inc., 156 Fed. App'x. 446 (3rd Cir. 2005) (unpublished), 15

Snyder v. Time Warner, 179 F. Supp. 2nd 1374 (N.D. Ga. 2001), 8

Speltz v. Commissioner, 124 T.C. 9 (2005), 62

Sullivan v. Sovereign Bancorp, Inc., 2002 U.S. App. LEXIS 8311 (3d. Cir. 2002), 15

Syverson v. FirePond Inc., 383 F.3d 745 (8th Cir. 2004), 16

T

Tanner v. Commissioner, 2003 U.S. App. LEXIS 7926 (5th Cir. Mar. 26, 2003), 64

Tatom v. Ameritech Corp., 305 F.3d 737 (7th Cir. 2002), 26

TVN Entertainment Corp. v. General Star Indemnity Corporation, 2003 U.S. App. LEXIS 3976 (9th Cir. Mar. 4, 2003), 46

V

Vague v. Bank One Corporation, C.A. No.18741-NC (Del. Ch. Ct. 2003), reversed and remanded (Del. May 20, 2004), C.A. No. 18741-NC (Del. Ch. Ct. Feb 1, 2006), 13

Varghese v. Honeywell International Inc., 424 F.3d 511 (4th Cir. 2005), 22

W

Walden v. Affiliated Computer Services, Inc., 2002 Tex. App. LEXIS 6396 (Tex. App.-Houston, 14th Dist. Aug. 29, 2002); withdrawn, substituted by 97 S.W.3d 303 (Tex. App.-Houston, 14th Dist. Jan 16, 2003), 36

Walia v. Aetna, 93 Cal. App. 4th 1213 (Cal. Ct. App. 2001), 29

Warner v. Warner, 46 S.W.3d 591 (Mo. Ct. App. 2001), 54

Wilson v. Bernstock, 195 F. Supp. 2d 619 (D.N.J. 2002), 43

About the Authors

Alisa J. Baker is a partner in the San Francisco law firm of Levine & Baker LLP *(www.levinebakerlaw.com)*, where she specializes in counseling individuals and companies on executive and equity compensation matters, including negotiating employment and severance agreements, representing founders in M&A transactions, and providing expert consulting services for equity-related litigation. Her book on equity compensation, *The Stock Options Book,* is the core required text for the Certified Equity Professional Institute (CEPI), and her articles have appeared in publications ranging from the *Wall Street Journal* to the *Journal of Taxation*. Speaking engagements over the last 20 years have included many appearances before industry groups including NASPP, NCEO, E*Trade, and SHRM. Alisa was a founding member of the CEPI Board of Advisors, and she serves on the MyStockOptions.com Advisory Board, the NCEO Equity Compensation Advisory Board, and the editorial board of the *Journal of Employee Ownership Law and Finance.* Alisa received her J.D. from Georgetown University Law Center and her B.A, M.A, and M.S.Ed. degrees from the University of Pennsylvania. She has been a teaching fellow at Stanford Law School and an adjunct lecturer in executive compensation at Golden Gate University. Before founding Levine & Baker LLP, Alisa was a partner with GCA Law Partners LLP, and before that practiced law at Wilson Sonsini Goodrich & Rosati and Fenwick & West. During 2000–2001, she served as executive vice president/general counsel of Snapfish.com Corporation in San Francisco.

Corey Rosen is the executive director and cofounder of the National Center for Employee Ownership (NCEO), a private, nonprofit membership, information, and research organization in Oakland, California. The NCEO is widely considered to be the most authoritative source on broad-based employee ownership plans. Corey cofounded the NCEO in 1981 after working five years as a professional staff member in the U.S. Senate, where he helped draft legislation on employee ownership plans. Before that, he taught political science at Ripon College. He is the author or coauthor of over 100 articles and many books on employee ownership, and the co-author (with John Case and Martin Staubus) of *Equity: Why Employee Ownership Is Good for Business* (Harvard Business School Press, 2005). He was the subject of an extensive interview in *Inc.* magazine in August 2000, has appeared frequently on CNN, PBS, NPR, and other network programs, and is regularly quoted in the *Wall Street Journal,* the *New York Times,* and other leading publications. He has a Ph.D. in political science from Cornell University, serves on the advisory board of the Certified Equity Professional Institute (CEPI), and is on the board of directors of The Great Place to Work Institute, producers of the "Best 100 Companies to Work For" list. The NCEO's Web site is *www.nceo.org.*

The material on the Sarbanes-Oxley Act in chapter 9 was contributed by **William R. Pomierski** and **William J. Quinlan, Jr.** Mr. Pomierski is a partner in and Mr. Quinlan is counsel in the international law firm of McDermott Will & Emery LLP, resident in its Chicago office. Mr. Pomierski is a member of the firm's Executive Compensation Group and its Tax Department. Mr. Quinlan is a member of the firm's Executive Compensation Group and its Corporate and Securities Department. Both have worked extensively with both public and private companies in the design and structuring of executive compensation packages, including stock and stock-based compensation plans.

About Levine & Baker LLP

Levine & Baker LLP *(www.levinebakerlaw.com)*, the law firm of this book's coauthor Alisa J. Baker, is a San Francisco firm specializing in employment law and executive compensation. It offers counsel both to companies (private and public) and to individuals. Representative matters include:

- Negotiation/preparation of executive employment, confidentiality, and compensation agreements (including equity compensation issues), including founders'/key shareholders' agreements, separation agreements, and settlement agreements

- Representation in trial and alternative dispute resolution proceedings including wrongful termination, discrimination, and harassment cases; compensation (including equity compensation) disputes; unfair competition and trade secret cases between employers and former employees; partnership disputes; and battles for corporate control.

- Representation of senior executives, company founders, and stockholders on their rights in merger & acquisition ("M&A") transactions and venture capital financings.

- Equity compensation plan/agreement design and drafting, and counsel on administration and implementation.

- Expert consulting and witness services in the area of executive compensation and equity compensation.

About the NCEO

The National Center for Employee Ownership (NCEO) is widely considered to be the leading authority in employee ownership in the U.S. and the world. Established in 1981 as a nonprofit information and membership organization, it now has over 2,500 members, including companies, professionals, unions, government officials, academics, and interested individuals. It is funded entirely through the work it does.

The NCEO's mission is to provide the most objective, reliable information possible about employee ownership at the most affordable price possible. As part of the NCEO's commitment to providing objective information, it does not lobby or provide ongoing consulting services. The NCEO publishes a variety of materials on employee ownership and participation, holds dozens of seminars, Webinars, and conferences on employee ownership annually, and offers a variety of online courses. The NCEO's work includes extensive contacts with the media, both through articles written for trade and professional publications and through interviews with reporters. It has written or edited five books for outside publishers. The NCEO maintains an extensive Web site at *www.nceo.org*.

See the following page for information on membership benefits and fees. To join, see the order form at the end of this section, visit our Web site at *www.nceo.org*, or telephone us at 510-208-1300.

Membership Benefits

NCEO members receive the following benefits:

- The bimonthly newsletter *Employee Ownership Report*, which covers ESOPs, equity compensation, and employee participation.
- Access to the members-only area of the NCEO's Web site, which includes a searchable database of well over 200 NCEO members who are service providers in this field, plus many other resources, such as

a searchable newlsetter archive and a discussion forum; a stock plan glossary; legislative/regulatory updates; and case studies organized by plan type and company type.
- Substantial discounts on publications, online courses, and events produced by the NCEO.
- The right to contact the NCEO for answers to general or specific questions regarding employee ownership.

An introductory NCEO membership costs $80 for one year ($90 outside the U.S.) and covers an entire company at all locations, a single professional offering services in this field, or a single individual with a business interest in employee ownership. Full-time students and faculty members who are not employed in the business sector may join at the academic rate of $35 for one year ($45 outside the U.S.).

Selected NCEO Publications

The NCEO offers a variety of publications on all aspects of employee ownership and participation. Following are some of our main publications.

We publish new books and revise old ones on a yearly basis. To obtain the most current information on what we have available, visit us on the Web at *www.nceo.org* or call us at 510-208-1300.

Equity Compensation

- This book, *The Law of Equity Compensation,* reviews and analyzes case and regulatory law developments in recent years.

    $25 for NCEO members, $35 for nonmembers

- *The Stock Options Book* is a straightforward, comprehensive overview covering the legal, accounting, regulatory, and design issues involved in implementing a stock option or stock purchase plan, including "broad-based" plans covering most or all employees. It is our main book on the subject and possibly the most popular book in the field.

    $25 for NCEO members, $35 for nonmembers

- *Selected Issues in Equity Compensation* is more detailed and specialized than *The Stock Options Book,* with chapters on issues such as repricing, securities issues, and evergreen options.

  $25 for NCEO members, $35 for nonmembers

- *Accounting for Equity Compensation* is a guide to the accounting rules that govern equity compensation programs in the U.S.

  $35 for NCEO members, $50 for nonmembers

- *Beyond Stock Options* is a complete guide, including annotated model plans, to phantom stock, restricted stock, stock appreciation rights, performance awards, and more. Includes a CD with plan documents.

  $35 for NCEO members, $50 for nonmembers

- *The Stock Administration Book* is a comprehensive guide to administering stock options and other equity compensation plans. It includes a CD with templates for immediate use.

  $50 for NCEO members, $75 for nonmembers

- *Tax and Securities Sources for Equity Compensation* is a compilation of statutory and regulatory material relevant to the study of equity compensation.

  $35 for NCEO members, $50 for nonmembers

- *Equity-Based Compensation for Multinational Corporations* describes how companies can use stock options and other equity-based programs across the world to reward a global work force. It includes a country-by-country summary of tax and legal issues as well as a detailed case study.

  $25 for NCEO members, $35 for nonmembers

- *Incentive Compensation and Employee Ownership* takes a broad look at how companies can use incentives, ranging from stock plans to cash bonuses to gainsharing, to motivate and reward employees. It includes both technical discussions and case studies.

  $25 for NCEO members, $35 for nonmembers

Employee Stock Ownership Plans (ESOPs)

- *The ESOP Reader* is an overview of the issues involved in establishing and operating an ESOP. It covers the basics of ESOP rules, feasibility, valuation, and other matters, and includes brief case studies.

    $25 for NCEO members, $35 for nonmembers

- *Selling to an ESOP* is a guide for owners, managers, and advisors of closely held businesses, with a particular focus on the tax-deferred Section 1042 "rollover" for C corporation owners.

    $25 for NCEO members, $35 for nonmembers

- *Leveraged ESOPs and Employee Buyouts* discusses how ESOPs borrow money to buy out entire companies, purchase shares from a retiring owner, or finance new capital.

    $25 for NCEO members, $35 for nonmembers

- *ESOPs and Corporate Governance* covers everything from shareholder rights to the impact of Sarbanes-Oxley to choosing a fiduciary.

    $25 for NCEO members, $35 for nonmembers

- *Executive Compensation in ESOP Companies* discusses executive compensation issues, special ESOP considerations, and the first-ever survey of executive compensation in ESOP companies.

    $25 for NCEO members, $35 for nonmembers

- *S Corporation ESOPs* introduces the reader to how ESOPs work and then discusses the legal, valuation, administrative, and other issues associated with S corporation ESOPs.

    $25 for NCEO members, $35 for nonmembers

Other

- *Section 401(k) Plans and Employee Ownership* focuses on how company stock is used in 401(k) plans, both in stand-alone 401(k) plans and combination 401(k)–ESOP plans ("KSOPs").

    $25 for NCEO members, $35 for nonmembers

- *Employee Ownership Concepts in Nonprofits and Government* discusses how nonprofits and governmental units, despite their lack of stock, can implement employee ownership concepts and build a more productive and satisfying ownership culture in the workplace.

    $25 for NCEO members, $35 for nonmembers

- *Employee Ownership and Corporate Performance* reviews the research that has been done on the link between company stock plans and various aspects of corporate performance.

    $25 for NCEO members, $35 for nonmembers

- *Ownership Management* draws upon the experience of the NCEO and of leading employee ownership companies to discuss how to build a culture of lasting innovation by combining employee ownership with employee involvement programs. It includes specific ideas and examples of how to do this.

    $25 for NCEO members, $35 for nonmembers

- *The Journal of Employee Ownership Law and Finance* is the only professional journal solely devoted to employee ownership. Articles are written by leading experts and cover ESOPs, stock options, and related subjects in depth.

    One-year subscription (four issues):
    $75 for NCEO members, $100 for nonmembers

To join the NCEO as a member or to order publications, use the order form on the following page, order online at www.nceo.org, *or call us at 510-208-1300. If you join at the same time you order publications, you will receive the members-only publication discounts.*

Order Form

This book is published by the National Center for Employee Ownership (NCEO). You can order additional copies online at our Web site, *www.nceo.org;* by telephoning the NCEO at 510-208-1300; by faxing this page to the NCEO at 510-272-9510; or by sending this page to the NCEO at 1736 Franklin Street, 8th Floor, Oakland, CA 94612. If you join as an NCEO member with this order, or are already an NCEO member, you will pay the discounted member price for any publications you order.

Name

Organization

Address

City, State, Zip (Country)

Telephone   Fax   Email

Method of Payment: ❑ Check (payable to "NCEO")   ❑ Visa   ❑ M/C   ❑ AMEX

Credit Card Number

Signature   Exp. Date

Checks are accepted only for orders from the U.S. and must be in U.S. currency.

Title	Qty.	Price	Total

Subtotal	$
Sales Tax	$
Shipping	$
Membership	$
TOTAL DUE	$

Tax: California residents add 8.75% sales tax (on publications only, not membership)

Shipping: In the U.S., first publication $5, each add'l $1; elsewhere, we charge exact shipping costs to your credit card, plus a $10 handling surcharge; no shipping charges for membership

Introductory NCEO Membership: $80 for one year ($90 outside the U.S.)